Personalisation in Practice

by the same author

A Practical Guide to Delivering Personalisation
Person-Centred Practice in Health and Social Care
Helen Sanderson and Jaimee Lewis
ISBN 978 1 84905 194 1
eISBN 978 0 85700 422 2

Creating Person-Centred Organisations
Strategies and Tools for Managing Change in Health,
Social Care and the Voluntary Sector
Stephen Stirk and Helen Sanderson
ISBN 978 1 84905 260 3
eISBN 978 0 85700 549 6

Personalisation and Dementia
A Guide for Person-Centred Practice
Helen Sanderson and Gill Bailey
ISBN 978 1 84905 379 2
eISBN 978 0 85700 734 6

of related interest

Person Centred Planning and Care Management
with People with Learning Disabilities
Edited by Paul Cambridge and Steven Carnaby
ISBN 978 1 84310 131 4
eISBN 978 1 84642 140 2

Personalisation in **Practice**

Supporting Young People with Disabilities through the Transition to Adulthood

Suzie Franklin with Helen Sanderson

Foreword by Nicola Gitsham, Programme Manager, Preparing for Adulthood

Afterword by Andrew Webb, President of The Association of Directors of Children's Services Ltd and Corporate Director, Services for People, Stockport Council

Jessica Kingsley *Publishers*
London and Philadelphia

First published in 2014
by Jessica Kingsley Publishers
73 Collier Street
London N1 9BE, UK
and
400 Market Street, Suite 400
Philadelphia, PA 19106, USA

www.jkp.com

Library of Congress Cataloging in Publication Data
A CIP catalog record for this book is available from the Library of Congress

British Library Cataloguing in Publication Data
A CIP catalogue record for this book is available from the British Library

ISBN 978 1 84905 443 0
eISBN 978 0 85700 816 9

Printed and bound in Great Britain by Bell and Bain Ltd, Glasgow

CONTENTS

Foreword

Last year Suzie and I attended a meeting of the National Children's Personalisation Network. A recurrent theme was that families and young people needed good information on what personalisation really is and how it can help young people move into adulthood with choice and control over their lives and better life chances. I had followed Jennie and Suzie's story with interest over the previous few years so was keen to see what she said. Suzie smiled and told me that she and Helen were writing this book and what did I think? My response was 'How soon can it be ready?'

This is a much-needed resource for families and professionals and is especially helpful at a time when people are considering the implications and opportunities relating to the new SEND (special educational needs and disability) system set out in the Children and Families Bill.

Young people and families tell us time and time again that transition is bruising and bureaucratic. We also know that disabled young people are less likely to move into adulthood with good life outcomes (such as employment, independent living, friends, relationships and community inclusion). The Preparing for Adulthood programme is building on learning from key national transition programmes such as Valuing People, Getting a Life and the Transition Support Programme. This book gives some fantastic examples of what we now know is best practice in transition to adulthood – for example, the following:

- Starting with the end in sight and thinking about what a fulfilling adult life will look like – too often the focus is on the next educational placement rather than the three questions posed in this book:

- What is possible for Jennie's future?

- What do we want for Jennie's future?

- What are we going to do to move this forward?

- The power of person-centred planning – Jennie's story beautifully illustrates the link between person-centred thinking and planning, person-centred reviews, personal budgets and developing Individual Service Funds. The book particularly highlights the importance of high quality person-centred planning and how to bring schools and other agencies together around a single plan.

- The role of personal budgets in developing creative and personalised support – the book dispels some of the myths around personal budgets and answers key questions raised by families.

- The need to support the development of circles – this is often the missing link for families and young people. Jennie's Circle played a key role in helping her to find a life she loves, providing support while navigating her way and making the most of natural and paid supports.

So this is why I have been eagerly awaiting the publication of this book! One of the top ten Preparing for Adulthood messages is that local areas should 'Raise aspirations for a fulfilling life, by sharing clear information about what has already worked for others'. Thank you Jennie, Suzie, Helen and Jennie's Circle for sharing your experiences. This book will help local areas to achieve this and ensure other young people and families have positive experiences of moving into adulthood and better life chances.

Nicola Gitsham
Programme Manager
Preparing for Adulthood
National Development Team for Inclusion
Oxfordshire
www.preparingforadulthood.org.uk

ACKNOWLEDGEMENTS

We would like to thank the many people who helped make this story possible. They are the other members of Jennie's circle of support – Dave Budsworth, Matt Franklin, Debbie Waters and Julie Bray (Person-Centred Review Facilitator); Barbara Mitchell (Service Manager, Stockport MBC); Joanne Baker (Senior Community Nurse, Community Learning Disability Team, Stockport MBC); Rob Henstock, (Managing Director of Independent Options); Joanna Babych (Team Manager, Independent Options); Jennie's team at Independent Options – Zoe, Dom, Hanna, Lizzy, Yvonne, Theresa and Heather; Chris Etchells (Housing Advisor, Independent Options); Caroline Boyle (Housing Manager, Jonnie Johnson Housing Trust); Louise Skelhorn (Person-Centred Review Facilitator); Owen Cooper (support to Jennie's Circle).

We asked some family leaders to help us write the last chapter of advice. Thank you to Gail Hanrahan (who leads family-led group Oxfordshire Family Support Network); Liz Wilson (Family Advisor with Dimensions); Debbie Waters (member of the Circle); and Marianne Selby-Boothroyd.

In this book you will read about person-centred thinking and planning. The person-centred thinking tools were developed by Michael Smull and the Learning Community for Person-Centred Practices. You can find out about the Learning Community on their website (www.learningcommunity.us). There is a summary of the person-centred thinking tools in the Appendix to the book.

Debbie Waters and Helen Sanderson developed the one-page information sheets for families.

Thank you also to Natalie Velos who helped us to get this book started, and interviewed Suzie to start to capture her story; Hilary Bradley for helping to edit an early draft; and Julie Barclay for designing the figures.

ABOUT THE AUTHORS

Suzie Franklin

I live with my husband Dave and we are enjoying the peace (and quiet) at home since both my children flew the nest. It took some getting used to but I take great pleasure knowing they are happy, active and independent adults.

My career changed direction when Jennie was diagnosed with autism…which seems a very long time ago. It became important to me to support other families of children with autism and this has become a huge part of my professional life for the last 18 years.

I made a conscious decision to work in the voluntary sector and retrained to help other families of children and young adults with autism to advocate for themselves and learn about their rights and entitlements. I have run training and parent workshops on a variety of topics related to autism, spoken at conferences and gained a Certificate in Professional Development in Autism Studies at Manchester Metropolitan University.

I am an advocate of person-centred planning and have seen the great benefit this can make to people's lives. Personal experience with my daughter Jennie has led me to train in some of the person-centred thinking tools described in the book to help families, local authorities and provider organisations strive for better support and services for people with disabilities.

I hope that families reading this book will be inspired to think that some of the things we have achieved with Jennie may be possible for their children.

Suzie and Dave

Helen Sanderson

I live in Heaton Moor, Stockport with my family, a dog, cats and hens. I met Suzie and Debbie through Jennie and her circle of support, and we have mutually supported each other ever since. I am part of a parents group in Stockport, and as part of the HSA Foundation, we have set up Community Circles to make circles of support like Jennie's available to more families.

Through my organisation, HSA, I have been part of leading the development of person-centred thinking and planning in the UK since the late 1990s. I was the Department of Health's expert advisor on person-centred approaches to the Valuing People Support and Putting People First Teams. I co-authored the first Department of Health guidance on person-centred planning, and the 2010 guidance *Personalisation through Person-Centred Planning* and 15 other publications on person-centred practices, community and personalisation. I am Director Emeritus of the international Learning

Community for Person Centerd Practices and have provided consultancy in Europe, Japan, Canada, Australia and America.

I hope that this book can help families see what is possible, and learn from Jennie and Suzie that there is a way for transition to adult life to be a positive experience.

1

An introduction to Jennie

Jennie is a young woman with autism and learning difficulties. This book tells the story of how she has successfully made the transition from living with her family to having her own flat and a support team paid for by a personal budget. Written by Jennie's Mum, Suzie, with Helen Sanderson, the book aims to show how person-centred practices helped Jennie and her family to achieve this goal. We hope that Jennie's story will inspire and inform other families who want their child to enjoy a full life when they reach adulthood. We hope that service providers and local authorities find this useful in working together with families to deliver personalised services.

In this chapter, Suzie describes the background to changes in provision for people with disabilities with the advent of 'personalisation' and introduces her daughter, Jennie.

Families like ours are currently facing major changes to the way support is being provided to people with disabilities. Recent governments have promoted a policy of 'personalisation' in adult social care, designing services around people and not the other way round, as used to be the case. For example, until recently, people with learning difficulties were typically placed in residential care homes where support was provided for the entire group. That kind of care could be very good but everyone had the same service whether they liked it or not – 'It's Monday, it must be swimming.'

Instead, personalisation means everyone having choice and control over the service they receive. Coupled with this policy is the introduction of 'personal budgets' which give people the chance to plan and purchase the support they need. These budgets can come in the form of 'Individual Service Funds', which enable families like ours to commission services from a suitable provider[1] rather than employing staff directly ourselves.

It sounds simple enough – and very exciting – but how can people with autism and learning difficulties, such as Jennie, have meaningful 'choice and control' over the support they receive and manage a personal budget? In my experience, finding out about and getting the right support can be difficult – there's a plethora of agencies to deal with and a complex system to negotiate. For families then, personalised services create a new set of challenges – how to get the best out of the opportunities now being offered. For providers of support services too, the issues must be immensely challenging, for 'customers' such as my family are now in the driving seat and organisations need to adapt their whole way of working.

This book is about how my family and Jennie's 'circle of support' enabled her to move from school into her own flat, with support workers of her own choice who help her to live the life she wants. The book sets out all the steps we had to go through to reach that goal, from thinking about the support she would need to finding her a suitable place to live and employing the right service provider. It shows how, all along the way, we used a set of practices known as 'person-centred practices' to help us define what we all wanted for Jennie and to plan and manage her support. But first, please meet Jennie and me.

For families, personalised services create a new set of challenges – how to get the best out of the opportunities now being offered. For providers of support services too, the issues

1 Think Local, Act Personal is a partnership of agencies that provide support and have come together to drive the personalisation agenda and promote good practice. They are the main source of information about personalisation – see www.thinklocalactpersonal.org.uk.

must be immensely challenging, for 'customers' such as my family are now in the driving seat and organisations need to adapt their whole way of working.

Introducing Jennie

Jennie is delightful 22-year-old. She is great company, fun to be with, has a cheeky sense of humour and a real zest for life. Jennie is creative and vibrant, has an infectious laugh, is bubbly, affectionate and happy. Jennie loves spending time with people that she has fun with, and she enjoys being active and often goes for walks in the countryside, especially anywhere near water. She regularly goes cycling at Wheels for All, trampolining, horse riding, aqua fit and Zumba! Jennie enjoys going out to eat and especially loves her puddings – just as well she gets lots of exercise! A very creative person, Jennie enjoys drawing, painting and making all her own greetings cards and gifts. She especially loves her iPad and watching video clips on YouTube, listening to music or trying out new apps. Parties and clubs, trips to the cinema and seeing musicals and ballets at the theatre are also among her interests. She has a very active and healthy life and also loves going on holiday with her family or support team.

Even though it is sometimes hard for Jennie to understand and express her thoughts and feelings, I admire her determination to communicate with us in her own unique way. You can tell when Jennie is happy by listening to what she says (reading between the lines) and watching carefully how she communicates and behaves. She is equally good at telling us when she does not like something or someone. Jennie lacks the social inhibitions that we have all learned and I admire the complete honesty in the way she just says what she sees, even when this can sometimes be embarrassing. In fact there are many occasions when I wish I was a bit more like Jennie, worried less about what other people thought and just said what I was thinking…

These are a just a few of the things that I love about Jennie but most of all I get great pleasure from spending time with her, watching her flourish as a young woman and seeing her enjoy her new-found independence.

Although I have always completely accepted Jennie the way she is, dealing with the issues her autism and learning difficulties have created has had a massive impact on me personally. The complete unfairness of battling for absolutely everything she has been entitled to and deserves has been a constant struggle and has taken its toll over the years. Having said that, Jennie has really changed me as a person, for the better I hope. I have learnt to be much more patient (not something I'm naturally blessed with) and absolutely determined as I have had to fight for everything for her – diagnosis, education, family support – and more recently the transition of moving her into her own flat. So having Jennie has undoubtedly made me a stronger, more determined, well-informed and accepting person.

I have had great support from my husband Dave and son Matt; we have supported each other through some tough times and had lots of fun as a family along the way…as well as a few tears.

Having Jennie has also changed the direction of my professional life and for the last 18 years I have worked for autism charities. I was involved in setting up a local charity, Leisure for Autism, in Greater Manchester and was a project coordinator there for seven years. For nine years I worked for The National Autistic Society, the last six of those as a family support programme officer which involved providing support, information, advice and training to parents whose children have autism.

Two years ago I started a new role with the Together Trust as a family liaison and support worker, based at Inscape House School, a specialist school for children with autistic spectrum conditions. Again my role is to support families whose children have autism and provide them with helpful information and ensure they know what their rights and entitlements are – this is something I feel very passionate about.

Figure 1.1 Family photo

My wish for Jennie has always been that she leads a happy, healthy, safe and active life of her own choice, with people she wants to spend her time with – surely something we are all entitled to!

In the next chapter, I'll explain how we gradually came to understand and accept Jennie's difficulties and our first steps towards planning her future beyond school.

2
Early years

Jennie's early years gradually forced me to acknowledge that something was different about my daughter. Painful though it was, getting a diagnosis of autism enabled us to get her the education and support she needed. And, luckily, during her school years I was introduced to 'person-centred planning', which made a big difference.

Jennie was born in January 1991. I remember looking at this beautiful baby thinking how lucky I was to have a healthy 16-month-old boy and a baby girl, little knowing what the future would hold.

Figure 2.1 Baby Jennie

It was my health visitor who first suggested that something might be different with Jennie because there were no signs of any reciprocal communication, such as pointing or involving others or language. But every time she raised a concern I dismissed it, partly because it was a denial response and also because I just could not see what could be 'wrong'. But as time wore on I had to admit there was something different about Jennie. Then everything seemed to change overnight and she went from being a seemingly contented toddler to one who slept poorly and appeared unhappy and confused a lot of the time.

By the time Jennie was about two her behaviour really started to challenge us. Jennie had very little awareness of herself or other people. If she wanted a drink she would grab my hand, drag me to the kitchen and throw my hand towards the fridge. I was just a tool to fetch what she wanted. The way she communicated was very impersonal and that was hard to deal with at times, especially as she wasn't using any words.

Other odd things also started becoming more noticeable. Jennie was obsessed with anything that was lime green and Thomas the tank engine, and she became fixed on routines. She would arrange her videos on the floor in an arc around her and if they fell over she would become hysterical.

One thing that really sticks in my mind is when she started to sit up on her own and I laid toys around her or just out of reach. This usually motivates babies to try to crawl because they cannot reach their toys. Jennie, however, showed no frustration at not being able to reach them, nor any motivation to try to move. As my understanding of disability at that time was limited, I tried to convince myself that she was just a late developer and some well-intentioned family and friends agreed.

But when I added all these warning signs together I began to accept that Jennie was not developing as she should and our health visitor referred her to the local hospital's child development unit for assessments, and we were seen by a community paediatrician. During our appointment she barely looked at Jennie, focusing instead on our parenting skills and marriage. I felt that we were the ones being assessed rather than Jennie. We came away feeling completely useless and that whatever may be different about Jennie was our fault. It was a very difficult time but we did attend speech and language therapy groups.

We were also told about an integrated nursery and enrolled Jennie, who by then was about two and a half years old. It was such a relief to meet other parents who were struggling like us. I asked the principal at the nursery what she thought about Jennie and she was the first person to suggest her difficulties could be autism.

I went straight to the library and took out the one book they had on the subject called *Autism: The Facts*.[1] I read it that night, thinking somebody had written a book about Jennie. It described everything about her with such clarity – the social, communication and interaction difficulties, the repetitive and obsessive behaviours. It was very hard to read because the hopes and dreams I had for Jennie were being challenged in every way and the future suddenly became a very different place.

Diagnosis

Reading the book made me determined to get a diagnosis for Jennie and I was frequently told 'we don't like to label children'. But I knew that without a diagnosis there would be no chance of putting the right education, interventions and support in place and these would be the only way that Jennie could reach her potential. I was determined she would get every bit of support she was entitled to.

Jennie eventually received a diagnosis of autism when she was three years and three months old. But I wanted more than a reluctant diagnosis and asked my GP for a private referral to a leading autism expert. The whole family went to see Dr Jonathan Green and he was the first professional I met who truly understood Jennie and what life was like for us. I didn't feel he was challenging my parenting skills and he started to take away the guilt I had been experiencing. This was a real turning point for me.

1   Baron-Cohen, S. (1993) *Autism: The Facts*. Oxford: Oxford University Press.

He produced a report about Jennie confirming her diagnosis but more importantly this has been the key to every bit of support and education that Jennie has had since. The report was like having an insurance policy for services. Jennie was four at the time and he recommended that she would need specialist autism education with small groups and specialist teaching staff.

> *I knew that without a diagnosis there would be no chance of putting the right education, interventions and support in place and these would be the only way that Jennie could reach her potential.*

School

We had been 'battling' with the local education authority to get the right education provision for Jennie but once we had this report, things became a lot easier. When she was five her statement of special educational needs recommended Inscape House School in Stockport, a specialist school for children with autism, which she attended from 5 to 16.

From 16 to 19 Jennie went to the Russell Centre, a post-16 education provision for young people with autism. It is attached to Inscape House so her education has been seamless. There Jennie learned the necessary life skills to help her prepare for her future.

An introduction to person-centred planning

When Jennie was about 13 I first heard about person-centred planning from a friend who told me about a course for families. Stockport Council had commissioned Helen Sanderson Associates (HSA) to run this course and it was my first step into the world of person-centred planning (see Figure 2.2). The course was led by a family trainer and co-facilitated by Julie Bray, who became a member of Jennie's circle of support. More about that later in the book.

Person-centred planning

What is it?

Person-centred planning is a way of organising around one person to define and create a better future. There are different styles of person-centred planning called Essential Lifestyle Planning, PATH, Maps and Personal Futures Planning. They all share a family resemblance:

- They all see people first rather than relating to diagnostic labels (although they are not specific to disability, they are used widely by people with disabilities, their families and human service organisations).

- They involve actively searching for a person's gifts and capacities in the context of community life.

- They focus on strengthening the voice of the person and those who know the person best in how they are thinking about their life now and what they want to change, and to move towards the future they want.

Essential Lifestyle Planning (ELP) was developed by Michael Smull and Suzie Burke-Harrison to help people leave long-stay institutions. It is most powerfully used in services, and the focus is on the here and now, rather than the future. From ELP has come a range of practical person-centred thinking tools, and one-page profiles. Families have used ELP to clearly define what is important to their daughter or son, and to assemble detailed information on how to support them well.

PATH, Maps and Personal Futures Planning are all graphic processes that focus on planning for the future. They were developed by John O'Brien, Jack Pearpoint, Marsha Forest, Linda Khan and Beth Mount. They each involve getting a group of people together around a person, with an independent facilitator, to create a visual picture or graphic. In PATH this is focused on a positive and possible goal and a plan to move towards this; in Maps the process includes identifying gifts and contributions and developing opportunities for community contribution. Personal Futures Planning is less common in the UK and the focus is to create powerful images of a rich life in the community and to search for opportunities for the person to take up valued social roles and develop service arrangements to support the person in those roles. All styles of person-centred planning are very useful for people who have personal budgets.

Is it policy? Has it been evaluated?

- 2001 Department of Health, Valuing People, was the first policy to mention person-centred planning.

- The Department of Health commissioned research into person-centred planning that was published in 2005 and established person-centred planning as evidence-based practice, increasing choice and having a positive impact on relationships and community.

- 2008 Department of Health, Putting People First, stated that person-centred planning should be mainstream. Good practice is described in the Department of Health guidance called Personalisation through Person-Centred Planning. This has a section on transition.

How can I find out more?

www.learningcommunity.US

www.inclusion.com

www.helensandersonassociates.co.uk

Figure 2.2 Person-centred Planning information sheet

As part of the course I was supported to put together an Essential Lifestyle Plan (ELP) for Jennie. An ELP is a style of person-centred planning to show what is important to a person and how to support them. Essentially it is a very detailed account of where someone is now and how they need supporting to achieve the best possible outcomes for them.

Initially I was a bit cynical about the idea of person-centred planning. I felt it was just another American fad and was concerned that local authorities and provider organisations would not 'get on board' with the concept. But as soon as I realised its potential I took it on board completely. Jennie's first ELP was completed in May 2004 with the help of everybody in her life who knew her best.

The plan started by introducing Jennie and describing what people liked and admired about her (for example, mischievous, affectionate, great sense of humour, full of energy), which was a wonderful way of describing her positively. It set out what was important to her (such as drawing and colouring, tickle games, visiting Chester Zoo and people she liked to be with), and what she must *not* have in her life (canned laughter on the TV, crying babies and dogs). There was a detailed section on how to support Jennie to keep her safe and how to communicate with her. The ELP has continued to grow and develop with Jennie over the years and is a constantly changing record of what is important to her and how to support her.

Everyone involved in Jennie's life has a copy of her plan. When she was at school a master copy stayed in Jennie's home/school communication book so that comments and suggestions could be added at any time by anyone who knew Jennie really well. It is really important that everyone continuously contributes to the plan so it remains accurate, reflects changes in Jennie's life and identifies areas that need action. We put together a one-page profile at the beginning of the plan (see Figure 2.3). This summarised what was most important to Jennie and how to support her, as well as what we appreciated about her. We used this with people who needed a snapshot of Jennie and how to support her, but who did not need to see the full plan; in effect a page of 'top tips about Jennie'.

JENNIES
ONE-PAGE
PROFILE

WHAT PEOPLE LIKE AND ADMIRE ABOUT JENNIE
Great sense of humour, infectious laugh, mischievous, lovely nature, vibrant, entertaining, determined, sociable, always finds a way to make you laugh, everything about her!

WHAT'S IMPORTANT TO JENNIE
- To spend time with her friends Alex and Rhian at weekends and in the school holidays.
- To draw, colour, stick and glue to make pictures from magazines, leaflets and boxes, etc.
- Loves to collect, flap and chew on straws.
- To watch one of her favourite Disney DVDs most days.
- When out and about Jennie loves to collect leaflets/magazines.
- Loves to listen to music, particularly in her room and in the car. Radio stations that play pop music, compilation pop CDs, 80s music and Disney CDs.
- Going to Chester Zoo, McDonalds, the cinema, the seaside, trampolining and horse riding.
- Going to Etherow and Bramhall Park as she loves walking near water and waterfalls.
- Jennie mustn't hear canned laughter/clapping on the television as this really upsets her. She sometimes gets upset when she hears crying babies.
- Jennie may need preparation before going to unfamiliar places (using visual supports or photographs).
- Needs time to process instructions, make sure you give her plenty of time to respond.

HOW BEST TO SUPPORT JENNIE...
- Jennie must be encouraged to hold hands/link arms at all times when outside, as she has very little understanding of danger, particularly traffic.
- If Jennie doesn't want to stop doing something or if she doesn't know what is expected of her, give short, clear instructions and use pictures and symbols to support what you are saying. Try 'First/Later' rule e.g. 'tea time first, horse riding later'.
- Should Jennie get stressed use short, clear instructions and key words. It may sometimes be advisable to use no language at all and show Jennie visually what is expected of her with pictures and symbols. Make sure you keep language positive. Tell her what you want her to do.
- If you need to move Jennie onto or away from an activity it is best to warn her and count down e.g. 'Swimming finished 5 minutes', '4 minutes', '3 minutes', '2minutes' and '1 minute' and then, 'swimming finished'.
- Jennie has in the past become very upset near dogs. However, she seems to be coping much better around them now.
- Jennie needs support and prompting with personal care routines and to ensure she eats a healthy diet.

Figure 2.3 Jennie's first one-page profile

I didn't want the plan to be stuck in a drawer and as everyone got into the habit of using it, it became a 'living' document about Jennie with scribbles and crossings out – 'Jennie doesn't do this anymore, she prefers this' – so we were constantly learning and everyone was keeping it up to date.

Jennie's first ELP included a lot of information on supporting her at school, on overnight respite and at home. Today, there is more detail on supporting Jennie to live in her own home; until she moved out I had a lot of information in my head because we did things without thinking. We had to write it all down so that other people knew how to support her. The plan is now hugely different from the first one back in 2004 (see Figure 2.4).

The ELP is a very effective person-centred planning tool for Jennie because people with autism need to be supported in very specific ways. Everything that anyone would ever need to know about supporting her is there, which has made a huge difference to the way she has been supported and the consistency of that support. Another important part of Jennie's person-centred plan is her communication chart (see Figure 2.5). This makes it really clear how Jennie communicates with her behaviour and how people need to respond.

However, it wasn't always easy keeping it up to date and encouraging others to use it because it was such a new concept for many people. Putting Jennie's ELP together took a lot of time, as does keeping it up to date, but it's definitely worth doing.

For Jennie, however, school years were nearing an end. What would the future hold for her?

> *The ELP is a very effective person-centred planning tool for Jennie because people with autism need to be supported in very specific ways.*

What is important to Jennie

Jennie's iPad and iPod available and working at all times.

Having straws and leaflets to hand and collecting them.

Having butterfly kisses and hugs when Jennie initiates.

To be listened to and have people respond to what Jennie says.

To have treats and ice cream when out and about.

Not to be rushed, go at Jennie's pace.

Having her own space when she wants it.

Jennie's things being left where she leaves them and not moved.

Spending time with family at weekends and seeing them some evenings for tea.

Knowing when she will see her staff team.

Being in control of what happens in her flat and Jen choosing what she does.

Visiting places like Chester Zoo, museums, theatre trips, cinema, the seaside, farms etc at least once a week.

Being active most days by going for walks in the countryside, horse riding, zumba classes, aquafit and trampolining.

Time to be creative at her flat every week go to local art classes and make pottery to decorate.

Spending time with her friends Rhian and Laura and eating out with them each month.

What those who know Jennie say they like and admire about her

Great sense of humour

Affectionate

Honest

Creative

Determined

Great fun to be with

How best to support Jennie

To have healthy snacks around for Jennie to have and to support her with portion sizes.

A visual timetable so Jennie can see what is happening now and next.

For people around Jennie to know and understand and how to respond to her communication.

Having time on her own and for staff to listen out to check Jen is OK.

Visual communication – gestures etc. (e.g. showing car keys).

Ensure enough time for what Jennie wants to do so that she is not rushed.

Plan well with Jennie and support her to do what is important to her and review any changes.

If unsure whether to speak – say nothing.

If you need to say something important to Jen, say "good listening" or " look at (your name)…".

Jennie Franklin

Figure 2.4 Jennie's current one-page profile

Where/what Jen is doing	What Jennie does/says	What we think it means	What others should do
Watching television or TV is on in the background	Gets upset when she hears canned laughter/people laughing and clapping Puts fingers in her ears	This is a real sensory problem for Jennie Not sure what is sounds/feels like to her but it causes genuine distress	Jennie is able to tolerate this noise slightly but will put her fingers in her ears and you need to turn the TV over or mute it for a minute You can also encourage her to turn it off herself
Anytime	If she hears someone say 'Come on' to her or someone else	Can sometimes get upset/ agitated and repeats it several times, getting more agitated	Avoid saying 'Come on' Try a jokey alternative like 'Let's go Jo' or 'Ready Freddy'
Anytime	Doesn't want to do/stop doing something or doesn't understand what is expected of her	She is frustrated She doesn't want to stop the activity	Short, clear instructions, key words Use pictures/symbols to support language and reduce stress Try the first/later rule – i.e. 'Tea time first, iPad later' but only do 2 or 3 instructions at the most
Anytime	Squeezes people too hard and can get over-zealous	She is excited to see certain people Being mischievous	Tell Jennie, 'Gentle hug/hands' or 'Hugging finished' or 'Leave me alone' and move away if possible If all else fails, tickle Jennie around the waist and she may let go

Figure 2.5 Jennie's current communication chart

3

Transition and person-centred reviews

Leaving school is a big milestone for any child but for parents with disabled children it's an anxious time. What are the options? Where will their child eventually live? Who will support them and how? How can we ensure their adult lives are fulfilling? This chapter describes how we started to plan for Jennie's future and how a number of person-centred practices helped us.

My concerns about Jennie's future and the transitions she would go through after leaving children's services were based on hard experience. When Jennie was younger I had to wade through local bureaucracy and fight to get Jennie, and us as a family, assessed for support from social services. It wasn't easy and sometimes I felt like giving up because it wasn't just a challenge to get support but it was a battle year after year to maintain what we had.

Once we had those services we just about kept our heads above water. We received four overnight respite breaks a month and direct payments which paid for four hours of support a week so that Jennie could use community and leisure activities that she would enjoy on a one-to-one basis. I knew that support in children's services was often easier to achieve than in adult services and that was a big motivator to start planning. I wanted people to look at what was important to and for Jennie and for her to be involved in decision-making about her life. I did not want her to have to fit into existing services if they were not suitable for her, which is what used to happen to people with disabilities.[1]

I worried about these transitions times and about the future for Jennie. Most parents who have disabled children will say their greatest fear and concern is 'What happens when I'm not here?' This was a huge driving force for me as I didn't want to be in a situation where I became too ill or old (or not here) to make sure that the right decisions were made with and for Jennie, let alone be able to care for her. It seemed the right time to start moving forward and the way we did this was to through a person-centred review.

Person-centred reviews

By this time I was getting familiar with some person-centred practices (like the one-page profile and her ELP) and saw their value in planning Jennie's future. The first person-centred review we did was a way of checking that Jennie's ELP was working, where we needed to look at it in more detail, and what actions we would need to take to do this. Keeping that plan alive meant reviewing it and Jennie's life. I knew it was important to get everyone together to start that review process, and for the first time this included Jennie too. Her first person-centred review was in November 2004 and we sent out invitations to everyone involved in Jennie's life and called it a review celebration (see Figure 3.1).

---

1 See a film of Suzie talking about transition (www.youtube.com/watch?v=7UiiSZ-JDy4).

To help to explain and make it attractive to Jennie we told her it was like a party, and used a building in the local community she knew well so that she felt comfortable. To make the event fun for Jennie we took colouring books, cakes, fizzy drinks and a portable DVD player so she could watch DVDs. Representatives from all areas of Jennie's life came along – family, friends, education, respite, transport, leisure, social services and the direct payments service. The invitations were used to prepare Jennie, with pictures of the venue, cakes, drinks and DVDs (these are detailed in Jennie's ELP as important to her so it wasn't difficult to get Jennie there!).

She loved it and jumped around and hugged people. And they talked about her differently because she was in the room. The person-centred review includes thinking about what is working about Jennie's life from everyone's perspective. With support from a facilitator, Julie, we celebrated the things that worked well and when things were not working so well we discussed them and decided how to make changes. These were then written in an action plan and people went away with responsibilities and timeframes in which to achieve them. If anything new or different came up it was included in Jennie's updated ELP. We agreed that we would review Jennie's plan every six months.

Jennie's review celebration

I'm really pleased you are able to celebrate my first person centred planning review with me

Because so many of you are able to come along it will now be at Stockport CP, Granville House, 20 Parsonage Road, Heaton Moor, Stockport, SK4 4JZ

4.15pm on Wednesday 3rd November 2004

These are the people who are able to come –
Me, Mum, Dad, Matt, Dave, Carol W
Jon and Betty, Social Services
Carol and Andy, school
Gill and Rosie, Swanbourne
Carol H, Support Worker
Theresa, Respite Carer
Geraint, Leisure Link
Lorraine, Escort
Jenny, SEN Transport
Barry, Direct Payments
Julie and Barney, Learning Disability Partnership Board

See you there, Jennie and Suzie

Figure 3.1 Jennie's invitation to her person-centred review

Person-centred reviews

What are they?

Person-centred reviews started in 2003 to answer the question, 'Can we develop a review process that takes the same amount of time, involves the same people, still meets statutory requirements, but is person centred in both process and outcome?' The answer was 'yes', and 'Essential Lifestyle Planning' (a style of person-centred planning) meetings provided the basis for the approach. Now they are used widely across a range of services and in different countries.

The first part of the review either records for the first time, or builds on, what we understand about what is important to the person and how they want to be supported. We then compare this to how the person is living now by asking what is working and not working from their perspective and others', and think about what else we need to figure out or learn. We look at what the person wants in the future, and what we can do to move towards that. The actions agreed should change what is not working, add to our learning about the person and move closer to the life the person wants in the future.

The process involves the person themselves, key people who have to be there to meet statutory requirements and, what is very important, anyone else that the individual wants to invite. They last up to 1.5 hours – no longer than a traditional review should take (although some people try to do traditional reviews in much less time). Here is a picture that shows the different headings used in the meeting.

Are they policy? Have they been evaluated?

1) A small study evaluated what people using services in the north-west of England thought about the person-centred review process and compared these with their experience of traditional reviews. People clearly preferred person-centred reviews.

2) Alison Wertheimer very positively evaluated the Valuing People programme of person-centred reviews.

3) Department of Health guidance (2010) recommends that person-centred reviews are used in transition and all adult services as a way to get started with person-centred change.

4) Many local authorities have already adapted their review paperwork and IT systems to reflect person-centred reviews.

How can I find our more?

www.helensandersonassociates.co.uk
www.youtube.com/user/helensandersonhsa

Figure 3.2 Person-Centred review information

Jennie's Year 9 transition review

When Jennie was 14 she became one of the first young people in the country to have a person-centred transition review. This was the same as her first person-centred review, but this one was focused on transition and led by education. We wanted it to be a person-centred review but we had to make sure that it 'ticked all the education boxes'. The review was held at Inscape House and we used visual supports to prepare Jennie for it.

Although Jennie's teachers had been at the previous person-centred review (see Figure 3.2), the actual education reviews had always been done separately so this was the first time they had been combined into just one person-centred review. It was quite a leap of faith for the school to go along with us because they had always done their annual reviews in a different way and we were trying to encourage them to work jointly with others so that there was no duplication of review meetings.

Helen and Julie jointly facilitated the Year 9 review and a few important things came out of it. In particular it was the start of us looking at planning for Jennie's future. When we had been developing Jennie's ELP a few years earlier, I realised that I was making all the decisions for Jennie and that the emphasis needed to shift so that Jennie could make some of those decisions herself, whether I liked them or not!

As part of the person-centred review we looked at Jennie's relationships. It hit me that Jennie's relationship circle included family but no friends (see Figure 3.3). Although friendships had not been that important to her I thought we had a responsibility to look at this. So we raised this issue at the person-centred review and asked everyone whether there were any relationships that Jennie seemed to be enjoying. Several people mentioned another pupil who had recently started at Inscape House. So Jennie's teacher asked her Mum to phone me and it was the start of a great friendship for the girls and also both families. Over the years we have met up on holiday, been out for meals, gone on trips out and have even been on their canal boat. For me, this illustrates how much the education professionals came on board with the person-centred review because something like friendship would not have come up as a discussion point at a traditional education review.

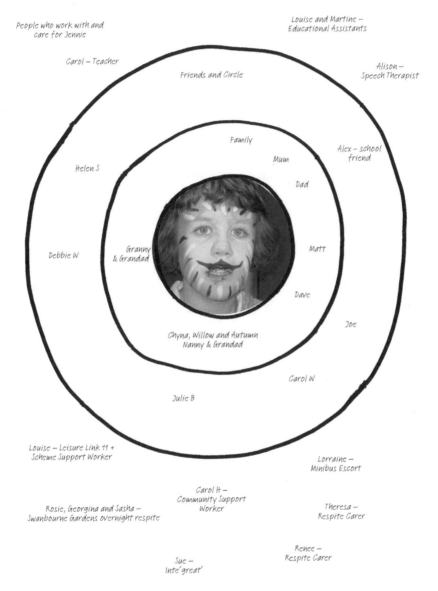

Figure 3.3 Jennie's relationship circle

Another issue raised at the person-centred review was Jennie's approaching work placement. I knew that she would not enjoy the options she was being offered, such as a placement in an office. Instead, we suggested that she helped out at a local riding school because she loves horses – horse riding is an important activity to Jennie and is detailed in her ELP. The school arranged it and she thoroughly enjoyed mucking out and feeding the horses, and even received a couple of free rides in return. It was much more geared around what worked for Jennie and what was important to her.

> *When we were developing the ELP I realised that I was making all the decisions for Jennie. The emphasis needed to shift so that Jennie could make some of those decisions herself, whether I liked them or not!*

Jennie's Year 10 person-centred review

Until this point, the person-centred reviews had focused on what was important to Jennie, and what was working and not working in her life, from different perspectives. Now, in the Year 10 person-centred review, we focused on the future. The review was structured around three questions:

- What is possible for Jennie's future?

- What do we want for Jennie's future?

- What are we going to do to move this forward?

The person-centred review was well attended and included family, friends, support workers, teacher, speech therapist, Connexions worker, social worker, social services team leader and manager.

Rather than use 'what's working/not working' as we had in the earlier person-centred reviews, this time Helen introduced us to thinking about what is possible in the future. We looked at this in relation to work, home, support and community life. Helen shared stories and examples of what people could do in each of these areas, for example, getting mortgages, paid work, circles of support, using personal budgets and really being part of communities.

Using flipchart paper, we wrote down which ideas we would like to see in Jennie's future. We used Jennie's one-page profile as a guide, reminding us what is important to Jennie as we thought about what that could look like in the future. Helen identified the major themes people had written down, so that we could see three or four clear areas for each key issue. Then she gave us all three sticky dots and asked us to put them on the areas we wanted to start working on straight away.

Some of the actions that came from Jennie's review were:

- thinking about Jennie's hobbies and interests and how she was spending her leisure time

- looking at 16+ education

- forming a circle of support (see Chapter 4) and

- thinking about future living arrangements.

I remember looking at everyone writing on the sheets of paper and jointly deciding what we should concentrate on to help Jennie. It was a really nice feeling knowing that I wasn't on my own and people were happy and willing to support Jennie and her planning process.

Reflections

Before the Year 10 person-centred review my main priority had been to get everyone working jointly to look at Jennie's transition from school to college and from children's to adults' services (and adult life), to look at the options available and try to ensure it happened as smoothly as possible. I thought we might touch on possible living arrangements for Jennie's future but wasn't really prepared for the extent of the other options, ideas and possibilities there were to think about and how differently things could be done.

I found the person-centred review quite overwhelming at first, because it really made me think that Jennie's adult future wasn't that far away and there was such a lot to do. But it was really good to know that everyone in Jennie's life was looking together at her future and planning with her and each other. It can be very difficult for parents to try to work through the maze of services and bureaucracy and find out what is actually available. So when people are working together and sharing ideas it definitely takes some of the pressure off.

I think it was good that most people at the review had previously been involved in gathering information for Jennie's ELP and had attended her previous person-centred reviews, otherwise they may have been a little overwhelmed at the different style and process involved in the Year 10 review. I also noticed that the group was definitely thinking in a more person-centred way, which was quite a positive shift from the way many support workers, service providers and managers have thought and practised in the past.

The great thing about both reviews was that Jennie was there, and so was everybody who was important in her life. Getting professionals to understand the benefits of this way of working was hard at first as they were reluctant to do things differently, but thankfully they did jump on board once they realised that having just one review made life easier for everyone. Both reviews made a huge difference to the way Jennie was included and talked about in a positive way.

Looking back, two things that came out of Jennie's person-centred reviews had a big impact on her future. The first was setting up the circle of support. Based on what wasn't working for Jennie at the Russell Centre, we learned that when Jennie left home she could live on her own and it had to be the right environment for her. At school Jennie struggled with the unpredictable behaviour of other students with autism and learning disabilities. And although the staff and curriculum at the Russell Centre were brilliant for Jennie, she didn't like the building itself because it was too dark and confusing to find her way around.

Person-centred reviews are more established now and all schools should have heard of them and I hope be starting to use them. Make sure that you know what a good review looks like (you can see one here on video[2] and see Figures 3.4 and 3.5), so that you know whether you are getting the real thing or a cheap imitation.

Getting professionals to understand the benefits of working jointly on a person-centred review was hard at first as they were reluctant to do things differently, thankfully they did jump on board once they realised that having just one review made life easier for everyone.

What does a good person-centred review look like?

A facilitator will support the person whose review it is to consider how they want to be at the centre of their meeting, and what it would take for them to feel as comfortable as possible to contribute their information and views and be as in control as they want to be. This also involves thinking about who they would like to invite to the review (for example, friends and family) and the people required to be there. Families also need an opportunity to prepare. They need to know what will happen at the meeting and what contribution they can make. It is vital that staff and professionals are there and contribute to the whole of the meeting, and don't just come to share some information and then leave.

Introductions – and contributing what they like and admire about the young person (written up by the facilitator on paper on the wall).

Sharing information

Usually flipchart paper is pinned on the walls in the room and everyone is given a pen so that they can write their thoughts on each in a more relaxed way. Another way to do this is around a table, with A4 sheets of blank paper with a question written at the top of each sheet. Information is recorded around the following questions (headings on the sheets of paper on the walls):

---

2   See a short film about person-centred reviews in schools: bit.ly/13rLSn3.

- What is important to (the person) now?
- What is important to (the person) for the future?
- What does (the person) need to stay healthy and safe and well supported?
- What questions do we need to answer?
- What is working and not working from different perspectives?

The 'What questions do we need to answer?' sheet is where people ensure statutory requirements are addressed. It is also a place to record any questions or issues that the person or their supporters want to work on or work out.

Agreeing outcomes and actions

Once the information has been recorded and shared, the next stage is to use it to explore any differences in opinion and generate actions based on what is working and not working for people and moving towards their desired future.

The questions that the facilitator may ask in this part of the review are:

- What needs to happen to make sure that what is working in your life keeps happening?
- What needs to happen to change what is not working for you?
- How can we address each of the 'questions to answer'? What else do we need to learn?
- What can we do together to enable you to move towards what is important in the future?

The next part of the process is to think about outcomes (where we want the young person to be in a year's time) and develop actions to move towards this. The actions should keep what is working and change what is not working. We also look at the 'questions to answer' and then think about any person-centred thinking tools that could help address the questions.

One action from a person-centred review is likely to be for someone to take the information and learning and either work with the person to create a one-page profile or add it to their existing profile to create a more detailed person-centred description. The record and information from the person-centred review is written up or photographed and produced in whatever way is required.

Figure 3.4 What does a good person-centred review look like?

How families can prepare for a person-centred review

What is it?

Families can prepare for person-centred reviews by looking at the headings in the review and thinking about what information they want to share under each of them.

These are the headings

- What do we like and admire about (the person)?
- What is important to (the person) now?
- What is important to (the person) for the future?
- What does (the person) need to stay healthy and safe and well supported?
- What questions do we need to answer?
- What is working and not working from the family's perspective?

Most families just make notes in a notebook that they can refer to at the person-centred review and write up on the posters.

Some schools and organisations create fill-in booklets to help families to do this.

Some families do this through drawing; for example, one father prepared for his daughter's review by drawing pictures that symbolised what he liked and admired about her. At the review meeting, he copied the pictures onto the paper as part of his contribution.

Other families have a pre-meeting with their family and friends who may not be able to be there. Mark helped Thomas and his family prepare for his annual person-centred review by inviting the people who knew him best, including family and friends. Using poster-sized paper and recording what was said in simple language and pictures, they helped Thomas map out what people like and admire about him – his positive characteristics; what is important to him; what he is good at and enjoys and some ideas for the future based on his qualities, skills and interests. This was then reduced to A4 size using the computer and shared at the person-centred review.

Figure 3.5 How families can prepare for a person-centred review

4

Jennie's 'circle of support'

Many parents of disabled children worry about what will happen to them once they are no longer there to care for them. Building a 'circle of support' for Jennie means that other people who know and care about her are contributing to her future in a meaningful way. This chapter explains circles of support, how they work and Jennie's Circle.

Many people with disabilities cannot articulate their hopes and dreams for the future, nor do they understand what their options are, but people who know them well have much insight to offer. A circle of support is a group of people – relatives, friends, professional carers sometimes – who come together to support a disabled person to positively change their life now and make plans for the future. We set up a circle of support to make sure that there were enough people in Jennie's life with the same interests and concerns for her future as me, who knew her well and who could help make the right choices about her future.

Who is in Jennie's Circle?

At the person-centred review Helen explained the purpose of a circle of support. I asked Helen if she would be willing to be involved and to be a member of Jennie's Circle. She immediately said yes. Being a member of someone's circle of support is a voluntary role, so we asked everyone at Jennie's review whether they would like to participate. The Circle started with family – Dave, Matt and I – and friends Julie and Debbie. Debbie is a close and valued friend and at that time a colleague. She has two sons with autism so brought a different perspective, as a friend looking out for me but also a professional in the field of autism. Another friend, Carol, who used to be one of Jennie's support workers, also volunteered and attends meetings when she can. Jennie's dad joined the Circle at a later stage for a while. It is a brilliant combination of family and friends who know Jennie well and have her best interests at heart. But also the Circle has good personal and professional qualities, particularly with Helen and Julie having person-centred and service backgrounds.[1]

How the Circle works

Helen led the first meeting and continues to facilitate meetings now. Helen introduced us to the principles of Positive and Productive meetings, and this means that we have a clear purpose for our meetings and agreed rules, and we use 'rounds' and share roles. It's very important to share roles so that everything does not end up on one person. When the Circle first started meeting, these were our roles:

- Dave and I were there to support Jennie.

- Matt was the timekeeper.

- Julie and Debbie provided food and drinks.

- Helen was the facilitator.

- We took turns to record meetings.

There were a few rules, such as:

- The meetings are to include fun and food.

---

1   See a video of the Circle at one of the very first meetings – *Jennie's circle of support* at www.youtube.com/watch?v=7UiiSZ-JDy4&feature=share&list=UUqflL4RfYI kK_ykYhVqNULQ.

- The meetings are confidential.

- Speak up and ask questions if things are not clear.

- Be honest and open about differing opinions.

- The meetings are to be held at our house.

Figure 4.1 shows our 'Circle meeting map' which we displayed at every meeting in the first year.

Figure 4.1 Circle meeting map

The difference the Circle has made

I was relieved we were sharing responsibilities because I felt so much was already resting on my shoulders with organising reviews and keeping the ELP up to date. Once Jennie's Circle was established it started to take that weight off me. Thinking about the future and how to make it happen is stressful for families of disabled children and the Circle helped ease that burden.

I think most of the time I have made good decisions with Jennie's best interests at heart but sometimes decisions can be made that are better for the parent and not necessarily right for the child. The Circle has enabled other people to challenge me in a safe way by asking 'Is that right for Jennie?' and that has been really good for me.

I wanted to see Jennie happy and settled and now the Circle means I don't have to worry about her because if I am not around I know they will continue supporting Jennie and everything we want collectively for her will carry on. The Circle will provide a forum to support Jennie the way I would like.

I would definitely recommend that other families have a circle of support even though it can be difficult to do. Our Circle has been phenomenally successful because of the combination of people involved and I know that it is not easy for everyone to achieve. Helen particularly has been the knowledgeable and creative driving force behind the Circle. I hope that other families and circles of support can use some of the things we have tried out.[2] Now 'Community Circles' are working to make circles available for many more families.[3]

> *I think most of the time I have made good decisions with Jennie's best interests at heart but sometimes decisions can be made that are better for the parent and not necessarily*

---

2 For another view of circles of support see Tomlinson, C. (2012) 'Love is simply not enough.' *Tizard Learning Disability Review 17*, 1, 26–31.

3 www.community-circles.co.uk.

right for the child. The Circle has enabled other people to challenge me in a safe way by asking 'Is that right for Jennie?' and that has been really good for me.

Thinking about the future – creating a PATH

Helen suggested we complete a PATH for Jennie within the first two months of the Circle starting.[4] A PATH is a style of person-centred planning that focuses on someone's future and how to get there. Initially the most important thing for me to concentrate on was Jennie's future once she left college and to think about the more distant future, for example where she might live, at a later stage.

The whole Circle was involved with Jennie's PATH, and it reflected the information from Jennie's ELP. We spent an evening with two facilitators using a visual process – a huge poster showing a PATH and all the things we would need to do together to journey along it.

We started off by looking at the future, called the 'North Star' – our hopes and dreams. Then we thought about what would be practical and possible in two years' time, then looked at the steps we would need to take in one year, six months, three months, one month and our first steps to reach that point. So, in effect, you start off by looking into the future and then work backwards to set the goals and deadlines to achieve that future. This is all written and drawn on the PATH (see Figure 4.2).

---

4   Pearpoint, J., O'Brien, J. and Frost, M. (1993) *PATH: A workbook for planning positive, possible futures and planning alternative tomorrows with hope for schools, organizations, businesses and families.* Toronto: Inclusion Press.

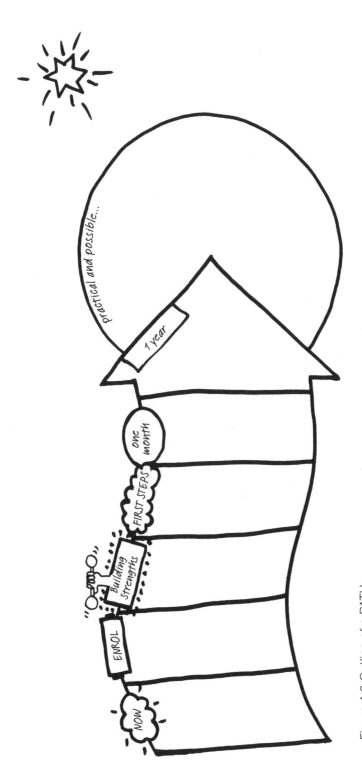

Figure 4.2 Outline of a PATH

Hopes and dreams

The facilitators encouraged us to be as creative as possible rather than focus on any obstacles that might be in the way. To start with I found some of the terminology a bit American – for example, 'North Star' – and I was slightly uncomfortable coming up with ideas that were too unrealistic because I was thinking 'Is that really going to happen?'. But using the PATH taught me that it is important to think really creatively because it encourages you to aim higher. Based on what we knew was important to Jennie, we came up with her ideal future scenario: she would be living in the country with animals, living close to a river with a waterwheel on the side of the house, with people who love her supporting her, near to a cinema and with a private jet to take her to Disneyland! Obviously this isn't going to happen unless (or even if!) we win the lottery, but the point is that this picture gives us a direction to aim for and to get close to it is an achievement. So, for example, Jennie loves being around animals and we are considering whether she can do some voluntary work at the riding stables or Chester Zoo. She is already a member of the zoo and goes at least once a month.

Challenges

The PATH was really useful because it kept us focused on what was important to Jennie and the possibilities for her future. But I personally found the PATH quite a challenging person-centred planning tool to use because I had to change my attitude from thinking 'This is ridiculous, it's never going to happen' to 'If you don't strive for the ultimate then you are never going to take little steps to reach your hopes and dreams.'

If you can change the way you think then you can change the way you support people. It's not necessarily about more time and money, it's all about attitude. The idea is to use the hopes and dreams as an inspiration and then work to a more realistic, achievable goal but it helps you think about things that may never have crossed your mind before. So although you can't make all those things happen all the time, you can get close to some of them some of the time. That is important and it sets you in a particular direction.

The PATH helped the Circle focus on what was important to Jennie and ensured we were keeping her at the centre of her life. The dreams we all knew were important to Jennie informed us about what activities she would do and who the best people would be to support her into the future. It was at the PATH meeting that we first started to think about personal budgets as a way to move forwards. The next chapter explains how we translated those hopes and dreams into practical reality.

> *If you can change the way you think then you can change the way you support people. It's not necessarily about more time and money, it's all about attitude.*

5

Jennie's personal budget and developing a support plan

With Jennie gradually becoming more adult, we had to face the agonising decision about when she would leave the family home and begin a more independent life. Where would she live? How could we put the right support in place for her? Would she cope? It was time for some serious soul-searching for me and time to learn what personal budgets could offer.

Jennie was due to leave the Russell Centre in July 2010 and our initial plan had been for her to carry on living at home with support. But over the previous months Jennie's behaviour had started to indicate that she didn't always want to be around us all the time; in fact she seemed to prefer spending time with her support workers, some of whom were only a couple of years older than her. We were also having quite a tough time at home with Jennie and it was the first time I started to seriously consider the possibility of her living away from home in the near future. It had always felt like something that would happen but only when she was much older.

Our new situation made me think perhaps it would be alright to 'let Jennie go' sooner. I raised it at the next circle of support meeting and it was a bit of a bombshell for the others. It was very emotional for me but everyone agreed that it wouldn't change anything we had been planning, apart from where Jennie lived, and it was something we should explore.

Moving into her own home was never going to be a decision Jennie could make completely on her own because she would never have been able to understand what it would mean. But with her best interests at heart, knowing what was important to her and with good planning, support and preparation, we could make it work for Jennie. The more I thought about it, the more I knew it was the right thing to do but I had to keep reminding myself of this as it was the hardest decision I had made in my life. Equally, I had to think about Matt, Dave and me too. Matt was at university and I really wanted to be able to give him some peace at home to study or have his friends round, something that had always been difficult for him when Jennie was at home.

Ideally after the Russell Centre Jennie could have had three more years of further education but there was nothing available that would have really met her needs. Everything that we knew was important to Jennie would rule out a generic special needs college as it would not have been the right environment for her and it wouldn't have the autism expertise she needed. Also what would she learn there that she couldn't be supported to learn in her own home and apply in a more meaningful way? And would it help her get a job?! There did not seem to be many options for Jennie other than staying on at college, but we wanted more for her than that – a future with work if possible.

I was also really worried that when Jennie left the Russell Centre or college the local authority would view me as her main carer. That would have had a huge impact on me and I would probably have had to give up work to take on that role. My main concern was obviously for Jennie, but the work I do is really important for me as a person; it had kept me sane over the years let alone paid the bills. I didn't see why I should give it up to look after Jennie full time. I was also sure Jennie wouldn't want to spend all her time with me either; it definitely wouldn't be what she would choose. I love

Jennie with all my heart and always considered what was important to her but I also had a right to think about what was important for me.

Caring for a disabled person is a huge responsibility and has a massive impact on you over the years. It affects every aspect of your life: having a social life, time to relax or even hobbies are almost impossible. Sleep (or lack of it) has been a huge issue for the family over the years and it's one of the biggest things that has taken its toll on me. Sleep deprivation affects your ability to function and just 'getting through' some days was an incredible challenge! Many marriages falter under the strain of having a disabled child and the effect on siblings is well documented. Often it is impossible for carers to work, especially single parents, so many families with a disabled child are on low incomes too.

So at the Circle meetings we started to work out how to move ahead with a personal budget so that we could find Jennie the right place to live, and support her to have the life she wanted. Personal budgets were a relatively new idea then, whereby social services give a budget to a family or individual to buy in the support they need themselves. It's very different from using one of their services as it puts the person in control but it can also bring the stress of managing a care package on behalf of someone.

For several reasons I didn't want to manage a team of support staff on Jennie's behalf. I had a very busy job myself and I was often working away so I didn't want the responsibility. What would I do if someone phoned in sick at 7am? Where would I get staff from at that time? Also, I wanted to be Jennie's mum, not someone who managed her staff with all the responsibilities, possible problems, paperwork and so on. How can you be impartial with staff when they are caring for your daughter? I was absolutely sure the best thing to do for Jennie would be to commission a service from a provider rather than take her personal budget as a direct payment.

When you use a personal budget with a chosen service provider it is called an Individual Service Fund. It means the following:

- The money is held by the provider on the individual's behalf.

- The individual decides how to spend the money.

- The provider is accountable to the individual.

- The provider commits to spend the money only on the individual's service and the management and support necessary to provide that service (not into a general pooled budget).

Figure 5.1 shows what it means in practice:[1]

Individual Service Funds

WHAT 'I can use my hours/budget flexibly and can choose what I am supported with.'

WHERE 'I am supported where it makes sense for me, at home and out and about.'

WHO 'I choose who I want to support me, my support worker knows me and I know them.'

WHEN 'I get support on the days and at the times that are right for me.'

HOW 'I choose how I am supported and my support workers know this is important to me.'

CO-PRODUCTION 'I am fully involved in decisions about my own support and how the wider service develops.'

Figure 5.1 Individual Service Funds: what, where, who, when, how and co-production

I wanted to be Jennie's mum, not someone who managed her staff with all the responsibilities, possible problems, paperwork and so on. How can you be impartial with staff when they are caring for your daughter?

---

1   Bennett, S., Stockton, S., Sanderson, H. and Lewis, J. (2012) *Choice and Control for All: The Role of Individual Service Funds in Delivering Fully Personalised Care and Support.* Available at www.helensandersonassociates.co.uk/whats-new/a-paper-by-helen-sanderson,-sam-bennett,-simon-stockton-and-jaimee-lewis,-showing-how-person-centred-thinking-is-central-to-individual-service-funds.aspx.

Getting started with a personal budget

Helen and I started talking to Jennie's Adult Services Care Manager, and the Commissioning Manager about Jennie being one of the first people in Stockport to have a personal budget (in 2009). Stockport Council were brilliant because, although personal budgets were still being piloted in the area, they were willing to let us devise a support plan for Jennie as long as they were happy with it financially and it met Jennie's needs.

There are six steps to setting up an Individual Service Fund. They are:

- allocation of resources (personal budget)

- planning

- agreeing the plan and contract

- implementing the plan

- ongoing learning

- regular reviewing of how it's going.

The first step was to find out what Jenny's indicative allocation was. Then we needed to build on the person-centred information we already had about Jennie, her ELP and PATH to develop a costed support plan (planning). Then the Council needed to agree this with us, and we needed to find our provider and put an agreement in place (agreeing the plan and contract). After that comes making it happen and implementing the support plan. Part of implementing the plan means learning and reflecting, as well as having annual person-centred reviews to review the support plan and how everything is going.

Jennie's indicative budget allocation

The Council had been working on a Resource Allocation System (RAS) to tell people what their indicative budget would be. The

RAS was based on a points system on which a cash allocation was calculated. The Council offered an indicative allocation that was still considerably less than funding the traditional residential service that Jennie would have been offered because of the limited specialist provider options available at the time.

The Council's view was that we would achieve significantly better value for money from the funding than a service commissioned by them. It is important to note that Jennie was breaking new ground from a traditional local authority perspective and the RAS was still a very new system so there was always going to be an element of trial and error. However, what this proved was that giving people greater choice and control gave us more flexibility to get a service that was right for Jennie.

Thinking about Jennie's support plan

We had 80 per cent of the information we needed for Jennie's support plan from her ELP and PATH. Jennie's ELP had all the information about what was important to Jennie and the support that she needed on a day-to-day basis. The PATH captured our hopes and dreams for the future. We based our decision on this, our collective understanding of Jennie.

Everything in her ELP and her PATH pointed to the fact that it was crucially important for Jennie to live on her own, supported by people who understood her, to keep her stress levels low. This then was our challenge – how could we use Jennie's personal budget to get her own flat, with her own support team of staff to enable her to have the best life that she could?

The Council needed a support plan that told them:

- who Jennie is and what is important to her

- what support Jennie needs

- how Jennie would stay at the centre of decision-making about her life

- what the outcomes would be for Jennie and how we were going to use her personal budget to achieve them.

As a Circle, we needed to think together about where Jennie could live, what she would do during the day, what support Jennie needed, and how all decisions would reflect Jennie, have her interests at heart and involve her as much as possible.

Where did Jennie want to live? Putting together our 'housing specification'

The Circle put together a 'housing specification' for Jennie, and knowing what was important to Jennie, we came up with a list of what was essential and what was desirable (see Figure 5.2). We worked with a housing advisor to help us, and we talk about this in Chapter 6.

Essential	Desirable
To live on her own with support staff – so to have a bedroom for staff to sleep over in	A garden
To live close to her family in Stockport – within a 10-mile radius of our house	A room to have time away from support staff where she can do her art
To live in a safe community, and for the house to have good security	Close to local amenities – cinema, swimming pool, train station, library, etc.
To part own her home – and have this security (rather than being a tenant)	
To have a light, airy environment to meet Jennie's sensory needs	

Figure 5.2 Our housing specification for Jennie's home

How did Jennie want to live? Putting together her 'perfect week'

We asked ourselves what Jennie wanted to do every week. Whilst we decided to get extra help to think about Jennie's future home, we knew that we could put her 'perfect week' together in a Circle meeting.

We started by doing a community map, which identifies all the places someone goes to at the moment, and places they might like to go to in the future (based on what we know is important to them). For Jennie this included local activities that she could be part of, places that she might want to visit and groups she might be interested in joining. We started with Jennie's ELP and looked at all the interests she had listed under what was important to her.

Jennie loves art and we started there. Most members of the Circle have some of Jennie's art in our houses, or on cards she has sent us. When we did her community map we thought about where she did her art at the time, and relevant local activities or groups that she might be interested in. Thinking about Jennie and art also helped us to consider what she might need for her house and from her future staff team. This was about more than keeping Jennie busy. We were also thinking about ways that she could potentially meet people and develop friendships. In the future, we also wanted to think about work and start to explore areas that she might eventually want to have a job in, if this would be possible. It was about making sure that she had a full, rich, active life and was spending time with people who were important to her; the sort of things that we would all strive to have in our lives.

We came up with the following:

- Jennie would need somewhere in her house to do her art, so we made sure that this was included in her housing specification.

- There is an art gallery in Stockport that she could visit and that also offers art classes on a Saturday morning.

- There are several colleges in Stockport and we could investigate whether any of these had art classes that she could join.

- Given what we knew about Jennie, how much time did we think she would want to spend involved in art each week – at home, and outside of home?

- Could we find someone to support Jennie who shared her interest in art? We added this to the support specification.

As well as where Jennie went – her community map (see Figure 5.3) – we also thought about who was important to Jennie. This was recorded on a relationship circle, which had Jennie in the centre, and then the people in her life in the circles around her (see Figure 5.4). We created her first relationship circle as part of her early person-centred review. We updated this as part of her support plan.

The inner circle represents the people who are closest to her – this is me, Dave, her dad and Matt. In the next circle are the people who are also important to her. The next circle is friends, and then the final circle is people who are paid to support Jennie.

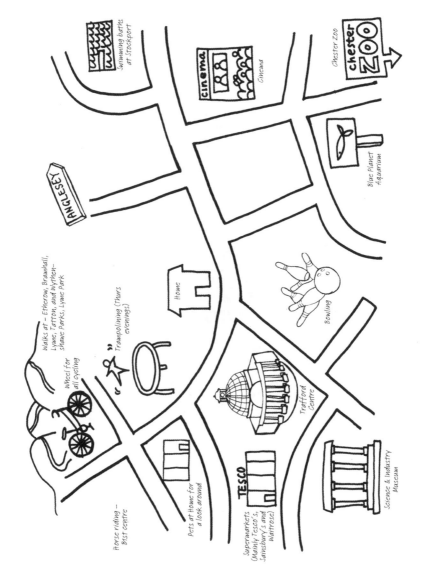

Figure 5.3 Jennie's community pap

Jennie's relationship circle

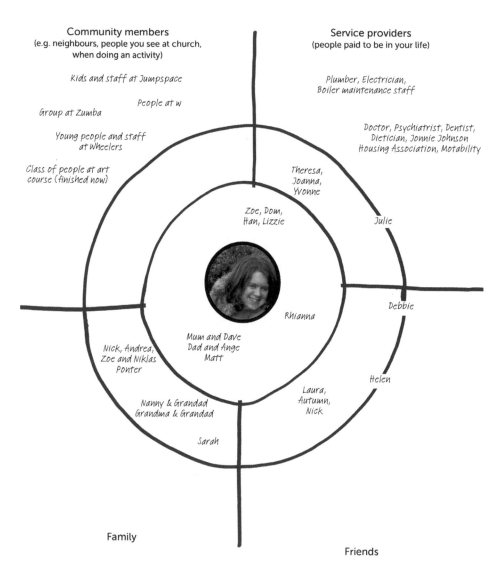

Figure 5.4 Jennie's relationship circle

As well as what Jennie may want to do during her week (for her 'perfect week') we also wanted to include how she stays in touch with the people who are important to her, and how and when she develops her friendships.

Once we identified a range of interests, places and hobbies that were important to Jennie, and her significant relationships, we looked at how we could incorporate them into a 'perfect week'. We took an A4 sheet of paper and wrote Monday to Sunday across the top and then 'morning', 'lunch', 'afternoon', 'tea', and 'evening' down the side. Then we slotted all the activities into a perfect week for Jennie, including a college course (art, music), dance class, going to the gym, horse riding, swimming and jacuzzi, cinema, bowling, trampolining, going to the pub for tea, spending time with family, seeing her friends, relaxing at home listening to music, being creative and watching DVDs (see Figure 5.5). Obviously this was more than she could do in one week, so this extended into her 'perfect month'. We added up what it would cost for Jennie to have a cinema card, entrance to a gym, classes, entrance to bowling and so on, to see what she would need each week.

As well as using her ELP, we also used her PATH to inform Jennie's perfect week by keeping in mind our ultimate goal of what Jennie's future should look like.

This was how we went from the ELP to the PATH, to the community map to the 'perfect week', and this trail of person-centred planning and thinking tools all ended up being incorporated into Jennie's support plan. Now that we had thought about what Jennie's perfect week and month should look like, the next step was thinking about what support she would need to do this.

> *We went from the ELP to the PATH, to the community map to the 'perfect week', and this trail of person-centred planning and thinking tools all ended up being incorporated into Jennie's support plan.*

	Mon	Tues	Wed	Thurs	Fri	Sat	Sun
AM	Gym or exercise class (Yoga?)	College course? (Art, cooking, music, life skills etc.)	Time to relax at home and listen to music, be creative or watch TV or DVDs etc.	College course (Art, cooking, life skills etc.) £25 (Supported through staff from ISF provider)	Time to relax at home and listen to music, be creative or watch TV or DVDs etc. £10 (Supported by Personal Assistant)	At Mum or Dad's	At Mum or Dad's
Lunch	Make lunch (Life skills)	Make lunch (Life skills)	Make lunch (Life skills)	Make lunch (Life skills)	Lunch at café or picnic	Lunch with family	Lunch with family
PM	College course (Art, cooking, music, life skills etc.)	Time to relax at home and listen to music, be creative or watch TV or DVDs etc.	Cinema, horse riding, bowling etc.	Walk, train to Manchester, Chester Zoo	College course (Art, cooking, music, life skills etc.)	At mum or dad's	At mum or dad's
Tea	At home	At home	At home	Tea out	At home	Go to the pub for tea	Tea with family
Eve	At home	Dance or fun exercise class	At home	Trampolining club	At home	At home	At home

Figure 5.5 Our first draft of Jennie's perfect week

How did Jennie need to be supported?
Putting together the 'support specification'

The support section of Jennie's ELP was like the job description for staff or anyone who needed to know how to support Jennie. Over the years we had developed this to be specific and detailed (Figure 5.6 gives some extracts from it.) So we already had the detailed information about what staff needed to do to support Jennie on a day-to-day basis. We now needed to work out how to stretch Jennie's personal budget to provide as much support as she needed. Jennie was assessed as needing one-to-one support and her sleep was often disturbed so we initially thought she would need waking-night support.

The Adult Services Care Manager provided information about how much the Council typically paid providers on an hourly basis for day-time support, sleep-in support and waking-night support. She explained the difference between a sleep-in and waking-night for us. When we put this information alongside the cost of the activities that Jennie wanted to do each week we knew that we could not pay for all of this from her personal budget. Although this was disappointing, we were still pleased we had started by 'thinking big' about what the ideal would be. Now our challenge was to see how much of that we could keep to be in budget and get just enough person-centred support for Jennie. This process is called 'Just Enough Support' and it means looking at the person's perfect week, and looking at where friends and family can provide support, where assistive technology could be used, and how to use staff time in the most flexible and person-centred way (see Figure 5.7).

> *Although it was disappointing that we could not afford everything we wanted for Jennie's 'perfect week', we were still pleased we had started by 'thinking big' about what the ideal would be. Now our challenge was to see how much of that we could keep to be in budget and get just enough person-centred support for Jennie.*

Jennie Franklin

This is Jennie's person-centred plan

Important people in Jennie's life have contributed their knowledge of and qualities, what is important to Jennie that details her many strengths, needs to know to keep her happy, fulfilled, active and safe.

To keep this plan up to date please jot down any ideas you have about things that might have been missed, things that seem to have changed, and your impressions of what is working well at the moment and what we might need to look at again. In this way we will be able to maintain the most accurate plan and use it as the centre point of all decisions that affect Jennie.

In time, and as Jennie's understanding of her plan grows, she will become more directly involved in making choices about how her life progresses.

Date of 1st plan: 16th May 2004
Dates of amended plans: 20th August 04, 2nd January 05, and 8th June 05

Thank you to everyone who has contributed to Jennie's plans

<u>NEXT REVIEW – TUES 19TH SEPTEMBER 4.15PM GRAINVILLE HOUSE</u>

Most recent changes are indicated in red, italic writing

What you need to know or do to support Jennie

- Jennie needs time to process instructions so give her time to respond (sometimes as much as 6 seconds) before you repeat anything or she may get confused and will have to start working out what you've said again.
- Keep language positive. Tell Jennie what you want her to do, e.g. 'Put the cup on the table' rather than what you don't want her to do, e.g. 'Don't walk around with the cup'.
- It is much better to say 'Finished' as opposed to 'No'. Jennie responds much better to positive instructions, e.g. 'Video finished'.
- If it's the last time Jennie can have something, e.g. a snack, drink or to watch a video, let her have it and say 'Last time'. Jennie will know she can't have any more and it's much better than her being told she can't have something when she expects that she can.
- If you need to support Jennie onto or away from an activity it is best to warn her and count down, e.g. 'Swimming finished 5 minutes', '4 minutes', '3 minutes', '2minutes' and '1 minute' and then, 'swimming finished'.
- Encourage and remind Jennie to get a person's attention by saying their name before asking them for something.
- Jennie finds it hard to comment on things she has done, as it can be difficult for her to understand the questions. Use photographs, pictures and symbols to help Jennie to comment on what she's done.

Supporting Jennie in the morning

- Jennie needs to complete her breakfast and morning shower routine before watching a DVD.
- Show Jennie her morning routine pictures. Just point/touch each picture e.g. bathroom and say 'Jennie Bathroom' walk out and give Jennie time to go to the bathroom, return and repeat if she has not gone to the bathroom.
- If Jennie seems a little grumpy don't talk, just point at the morning routine.
- Jennie prefers to have a shower in the morning. Please tie Jennie's hair up so it doesn't get too wet. There is a bobble in the bathroom.
- Jennie needs encouragement to clean her teeth properly. She has a two-minute timer which she is happy to use without much protesting. You may need to model teeth cleaning when Jennie is cleaning her teeth as she tends to rush or not clean her teeth properly!
- Jennie's face is spotty at times and, with support, she is cleansing with Sensitive Skin Wipes morning and night. She needs prompting to ensure she cleans around the nose, forehead and chin.

Figure 5.6 Extracts from the support section of Jennie's ELP

Just Enough Support

What is it?

'Just Enough Support' means the optimum level of support that will increase the chances of people connecting with local people in their communities.

If we use resources effectively and actively reduce reliance on paid support, while working in ways that enhance relationships and involve people in their community, then we can achieve a 'win-win' situation for:

- the person – who will have a wider variety of connections and relationships
- the organisation – which will be able to target scarce resources most effectively, and
- the community – which will benefit from the contributions and presence of disabled people.

There are four stages to providing just enough support: generating ideas, testing them (Do they work for the person? Do they provide enough support?), trying them in practice and reviewing them. To generate ideas, we first of all clearly identify what, how much and when the person needs support, then think about three possible ways of providing it – starting with people in the person's network and in the community, then assistive technology and finally paid staff.

The process involves a group that can generate ideas, to then check and test out with the person if they do not want to be part of this group. The group thinks together about how to deliver the support the person needs to have their 'perfect week'. Here are the four questions that the group look at:

1) Exactly what support does the person need?

    The group accurately describe exactly what support the person needs, how much and how often, not how it is currently provided.

2) Are there other people or community initiatives that could help?

    You would use the person's relationship map and community map (both person-centred thinking tools) to look at whether family or friends could help, then look at community initiatives like Timebanks.

3) Could assistive technology help?

4) Are there ways we could think differently about paid support?

There are different models of support to consider here, for example, community service volunteers, the Keyring model (www.keyring.org), zero hours contracts to offer maximum flexibility, or 'life sharing' possibilities.

These ideas are tested with the individual (Do they reflect what is important to you? Do they deliver just enough support?), and then put into practice. Where paid staff are needed, they are matched to the individual, and this information is put into a personalised rota. Everything is reviewed through a person-centred review.

How can I find out more?

www.imagineactandsucceed.co.uk
www.helensandersonassociates.co.uk
www.youtube.com/user/helensandersonHSA

Just Enough Support was developed by I.A.S and H.S.A, building on the work described in the paper 'All Together Now'.

Figure 5.7 – Just Enough Support information

We started by looking at what family or friends could contribute to supporting Jennie. One way to reduce the cost was to look for a provider for five days a week only and for Jennie to spend the weekends with us, or with her dad. We decided that this was a win-win option. It meant that we could see a lot of Jennie on our own, but still have weekends to ourselves (Jennie's dad and Dave and I planned to do alternate weekends) and it meant that Jennie's budget would go further.

We could not see how we could use assistive technology to support Jennie. The final part of thinking about Just Enough Support was to consider how to use staff time well. We realised that the other way we could save money was to see if Jennie would get enough support with a sleep-in rather than the waking-night support that we had assumed she would need. We started by recording Jennie's sleep patterns and adapted a 'learning log' (see Appendix) to capture this information. We did this for a month until the next Circle meeting when we came back together to finish Jennie's support plan.

At this meeting we looked at Jennie's sleep records. We thought that she just needed sleep-in support, but we were worried that with the big change of moving to her own place and having new staff, her sleep would be more disturbed and she would need waking-night support. We talked this through with the Care Manager, who came to the Circle meeting to help us think about this. We agreed that as soon as reasonable we would move staff onto a sleep-in rota and that the Council would initially pay us additional money to cover waking-night staff. The Care Manager was clear that this could only be for the first three months but she also agreed a contingency fund of £2500 in the first year to support any additional hours when staff might be disrupted at night if Jennie did wake up.

Therefore, we would be looking for one-to-one support for Jennie for five days a week plus sleep-in support (but waking-night allowance for staff). This would then leave enough money in Jennie's personal budget to cover the money she needed for her perfect week.

Now we knew what we wanted the provider to support Jennie to do (her perfect week), how much time we needed them for, and what exactly they needed to do to support Jennie. We were looking for person-centred support from a provider and this included keeping Jennie at the centre of decisions about her life, and working closely with the Circle. To complete the support plan we needed to look at how Jennie could stay at the centre of decision-making about her life and support.

How could Jennie stay at the centre of these decisions? Putting together a decision-making agreement

Jennie already had a communication chart (see Figure 2.5) as part of her ELP. This clearly tells people how Jennie communicates with her behaviour, and most importantly, what it means and how we want people to respond. Now we wanted to develop this further and share with people how Jennie could be part of and central to decisions in her life. This is called a decision-making agreement. I developed this with help from Julie and then shared it with the rest of the Circle to check (see Figure 5.8).

Jennie's decision-making profile

How I like my information	How to present choice to me	How you can help me understand	When are the best times to ask me to make decisions	When it is not a good time to ask me to make decisions
Use very simple and clear instructions Only use the most important words Use visual schedules and Social Stories™ Give me time to think about what you are asking	If it's something I am familiar with then you may be able to give me a simple, verbal choice If it is something unfamiliar then it is better to use visual cues/pictures etc.	Use a visual social story to help me understand what it is you want me to make a decision about If I struggle with this my family know me really well and will be able to help Check I understand (although you may have to ask people who know me really well)	When I am in a 'happy mood' and enjoying being around others After meals when I'm not hungry At home when I'm downstairs and not doing a favourite activity (on the computer or painting)	Not in my bedroom as I don't usually like being disturbed when listening to music or reading When I am starting to get unhappy and wound up Not after I have been upset or unhappy Not first thing in the morning

My important decisions and how I make them

Decisions in my life	How I must be involved and who can help	Who makes the final decision
What I eat	Mum usually plans and makes the family meals but she knows what food I like (it's in my plan) when I am at my family home At home with my PAs I will choose, prepare and make my lunch – I really like doing this I like to choose my snacks I have a visual healthy eating plan to help me make healthy choices and not eat too much and know that I can have three treats every week. Family and people who support me help me with this	Jennie as much as possible at her flat, and Suzi when Jennie visits the family home
Where I go in the day	The Circle has put together a 'perfect week' based on what I enjoy doing My staff will use learning logs to review what works and does not work about my weekly plan Sometimes I get stressed making decisions so I prefer it when people who know me really well make decisions for me. I know they will choose something they know I like	The Circle has suggested activities. Jennie will decide on a day-by-day basis what she does with support from her staff
Who I'm friends with	I met the friends I have through family, at school, college and trampolining club I like to be in a familiar place and with people who know me really well to make friends I like to choose my friends but this can take a long time I may not speak much to them but I still like being with them Family members make sure I get time to spend with my friends, and my staff will support me in this as well	Jennie

Figure 5.8 Jennie's decision-making agreement

Pulling this together into 'outcomes' and costing the support plan

We were then at the stage of pulling this all together into 'outcomes' for the support plan. The support plan had to be signed off by the Council and in our case this was by the Care Manager.

We took an 'outcome' to be what we wanted Jennie's life to be like in a year's time. We wanted Jennie to:

- have a full week, as close to her 'perfect week' as possible, so that she could take part in local leisure activities, at her pace, with the support she needed

- stay with/see her mum and Dave and her dad at the weekends

- move into her own flat with the support she needed

- be supported by a team providing 'Jennie-centred support' so that she could be healthy and safe.

We also wanted the Circle and support team to keep learning and thinking about Jennie's future and exploring work and volunteering possibilities.

We wanted this to be achieved by working with a provider to manage Jennie's money as an Individual Service Fund, so that the family and Circle did not have to administer it and could support Jennie in other ways. We wrote this into Jennie's support plan.

In the next chapter we explain how we found the right accommodation for Jennie – a critical factor in supporting her to enjoy 'her perfect week'.

6
Finding Jennie a place to live

Finding Jennie the right place to live was always going to be a challenge. Even so, we seriously underestimated the time it would take and the financial and legal complexities of setting Jennie up in her own home.

We thought about lots of housing options for Jennie. The first was private renting, but we discounted this because it wouldn't be Jennie's place and a landlord could sell up at any time and ask Jennie to leave. She would need continuity and stability wherever she was going to live. We also looked at council housing but, bearing in mind how vulnerable Jennie is, we were concerned about the areas she might be offered. The last option was shared ownership, which is a way of buying a percentage of a property and renting the rest. We believed this would be best for Jennie because it gave her a share in her own home.

The Circle, Jennie's Care Manager and I looked into shared ownership and a few days later the manager called to say that a recently completed housing association project, provided by Johnnie Johnson Housing Trust (a social housing provider) still had a couple of flats on the market. Amazingly it was only a couple of miles from our house and in an area Jennie was familiar with, so the location couldn't have been better. At this point it was July 2009 and it was still a year away from when Jennie would leave the Russell Centre so I thought it was a bit soon to be looking. But the

Care Manager persuaded me that these things take time – and I'm very glad she did!

The building had 14 flats and there was just one left on the market, which had three bedrooms. Dave and I went to view the flat and as soon as we walked in I could picture Jennie living there; it was gorgeous – very spacious and light, which would really work well with Jennie's sensory processing difficulties. The extra bedroom meant Jennie could have an art, craft and music room and somewhere to 'escape to' if she wanted to be on her own, which she needs quite a bit of the time.

We had already decided to get advice from Chris Etchells, a housing advisor who worked for a local provider called Independent Options, on how we would finance the flat and whether it would be a good option for Jennie. We needed to make sure Jennie could afford to do this; she had to be financially independent because we couldn't afford to support her if she lived away from home. Chris put us in touch with a specialist mortgage broker, My Safe Home, who arranged mortgages for people with disabilities to live in their own homes. He explained that because Jennie was on income support she would be eligible for a mortgage support payment, on top of her income support. The Department for Work and Pensions had to agree that Jennie was entitled to this additional payment, which would cover the interest on her mortgage payments. As the mortgage she was applying for was an interest-only one, the monthly payments would be covered this way. She was also entitled to housing benefit which would cover the rent and the service charge on the other 50 per cent of the flat.

Once we had checked all the finances would work for Jennie and everyone was in agreement that the shared ownership flat was the best option for Jennie, we filled in an application form, paid a deposit, and it was Jennie's. And then the hard work began…

Jennie doesn't have the mental capacity to understand what a contract is and consequently could not sign a mortgage agreement. In my naivety I thought I could just sign it for her. I didn't realise that I would have to apply to the Court of Protection to become

Jennie's legal deputy. This opened up a massive complication that I had never anticipated. I soon learned that being a deputy is similar to having power of attorney, except the latter is made by the person before they lose mental capacity and a deputyship application is made by a third party when the individual has no mental capacity or after they have lost capacity.

We had only a certain number of weeks before the mortgage offer expired so I went on the Court of Protection website and looked at all the forms in horror. I downloaded them and drafted answers but it was so complicated that at one stage I didn't know whether to cry or rip them all up and start again. I just kept thinking that delay could mean losing the flat and it was the last one left with no other shared ownership schemes available or planned in Stockport.

We applied for an interim order because it can take 9–12 months for the deputy process to go through the Court of Protection and we just didn't have that much time. I must have spent about 20 hours filling in forms because it is still not over when you send your application in. Jennie's Care Manager filled in the forms relating to Jennie's mental capacity and whether she could understand and sign an agreement or not. When the Court of Protection acknowledge your application, you have to 'serve people on your intention for deputyship' and then fill in more forms saying who you have served and when and how you served them. You repeat the process when the interim order is granted, and again when the final order comes through. It was pretty horrendous to be honest. The interim order finally came through in the middle of November 2009 and the mortgage was approved just before Christmas.

We had to pay a deposit for the flat, £400 to the Court of Protection for the deputyship order, arrangement fees for the mortgage broker and the mortgage lender's and solicitor's fees, so it was an expensive process. In addition to this we also had to carpet and furnish the flat. This totalled several thousand pounds, which could be prohibitive for many families. We were very lucky as a close friend left me some money in her will and this enabled us to set Jennie up in the flat. It was worth spending every penny to give Jennie her independence.

With Jennie's home secure we could finalise the decision about a provider to deliver her support, as the next chapter shows.

> *I downloaded the Court of Protection forms and drafted answers but it was so complicated that at one stage I didn't know whether to cry or rip them all up and start again. I just kept thinking that delay could mean losing the flat.*

7
Finding a service provider

At the same time as deciding where Jennie would live we had to find the right organisation to provide Jennie's support so she could live in her own home with the right support. Our first consideration was whether we needed an autism expert or a provider prepared to become a 'Jennie expert'.

We started by getting recommendations of providers from people we knew. This gave us four potential services providers in the area, two being providers specialising in providing support for people with autism.

Autism expert or Jennie expert?

Originally I wanted Jennie to be supported by an autism-specific service provider because this is what she has always needed. However, in discussions with the Circle Helen suggested that the right person-centred organisation would provide 'Jennie-specific' support. We agreed that we could use some of Jennie's budget to provide autism training for the team or even buy in some specialist consultancy if required, but that it would be much better for Jennie if her team were the specialists in supporting her. I really did struggle with this at first but the more I thought about it and the options we had open to us, the more it made sense. We had so much information in Jennie's ELP about what people needed to do to provide the best support for her and we needed to feel confident that a provider was committed to delivering this, whether they had autism experience or not.

'Interviewing' providers

Different members of the Circle made a first contact with each of the providers to see if they were interested in principle in supporting Jennie through an Individual Service Fund. They all said that they were. Next we sent them some information about Jennie (her one-page profile and her 'perfect week') and asked them to send us their risk policy. We thought that seeing an organisation's risk policy would provide an insight into whether they were working in person-centred ways or not. You can tell a lot about an organisation's culture by how it approaches risk. One way to find out how person centred an organisation is, is to look at their approach to risk. One of the providers refused to send us their risk policy, so we were then down to three providers.

We thought together in the Circle about what we wanted to ask each provider, and put this together as a kind of interview schedule (see Figure 7.1). We asked questions about how they would support Jennie first, then how they would work with the Circle, and how we would be involved in recruiting Jennie's staff, and finally, about the organisation.

We then either visited or invited each of the three remaining providers to a Circle meeting and were armed with the questions to make sure they all had the same opportunity to provide us with information. It was interesting to note whether the organisation sent a senior or a more junior manager. We asked Independent Options back for a second interview and they sent the then Chief Executive, Rob Henstock, who filled us with confidence. Meeting the person who would be the manager of Jennie's service, as well as the CEO, helped us make our decision.

Questions for providers
Focus on Jennie Do they see Jennie as a person, and pay attention to who she is (as described in her person-centred plan)?
Do we think they can support Jennie in the specific, detailed way she needs (be Jennie experts, informed by her autism)?
Can they deliver Jennie's perfect week? All of it? Some of it? What gets in the way?
Working towards Jennie's future – do we feel they will work with us in a creative way to explore what the future could look like for Jennie (moving towards dreams)?
Working with the family and Circle Do we think that they will respect the family and Circle as decision makers?
Can the Circle make the final decisions in recruiting staff?
Will they recruit the people we have already identified to support Jennie?
Supervising and supporting staff Are we confident about how they know how staff are doing (spending time with staff, not relying on what staff say) Do staff receive monthly support/supervision sessions – are we impressed with what happens there? Do staff have regular team meetings (every 6 weeks) and what is the content? How do they manage risk? What is their turnover rate? What is their sickness rate?
Leadership in the organisation Do we think we could work with the lead person? Do they inspire confidence? Does the leader (most senior manager) inspire us with their values and practices? Do they feel like a person-centred organisation – how do we know? Have they been efficient in their communication and relationship with us so far?
Finances How do the hourly rates compare? Is there any flexibility in how the money is used? Do we think they will work with us to make Jennie's money go as far as possible?

Figure 7.1 Our interview questions for providers

Reaching a decision was easy because Independent Options was by far top of the list in every aspect. They came prepared, supplied extra information willingly and promptly, and were willing to work with the Circle in an open and honest way. This was the first time they had been commissioned by a circle of support and whenever there has been an issue about the contract or costs or when things haven't gone to plan, they have always been happy to sit down with us and resolve it.

The next step was to work with Independent Options to find the best staff for Jennie.

> One way to find out how person centred an organisation is, is to look at their approach to risk. One of the providers refused to send us their risk policy. This told us we did not want them to support Jennie.

8

Getting the right staff for Jennie

Choosing the right staff for Jennie was one of the most important decisions to make and the Circle wanted to make sure that she was at the centre of this. We decided that the best way to involve Jennie was to do the recruitment in partnership with the provider.

Many organisations simply have several people who use their service trained and supported to sit on recruitment panels in the organisation. We knew that this would not be the answer for Jennie. To keep Jennie at the centre of selecting staff meant that we needed to start with the person specification and job description, and make sure that this was Jennie specific. I think Independent Options thought that we would simply use their existing job descriptions and amend them for Jennie, but we had other ideas!

The person specification, job description and advert

We used the person-centred thinking tool 'Matching staff' (see Figure 8.1 and Appendix) to think about the kind of person who would be the best match for Jennie. We used her ELP, picking out the characteristics that someone who worked with Jennie would need. This meant thinking about the support Jennie needed, the skills that someone would need, what kind of person they would need to be (personality characteristics) and what kind of interests they should share with Jennie. There was no point in choosing someone who didn't like horses because they wouldn't want to take her riding, and the same went for Jennie's other interests such as swimming and going for walks. This gave us the 'person specification' (see Figure 8.1).

Next we needed the job description (see Figure 8.2) This was also easy to take from the ELP. Alongside this we used a person-centred thinking tool called the Doughnut. This is a way to clarify roles and responsibilities. The job description was written in three parts covering what we expected from staff in relation to:

- Jennie herself

- the family and Circle

- the organisation.

This is a different way to write a job description. The order felt important to us. We wanted to be clear right from the beginning with anyone who might work with Jennie, that their primary responsibility was to Jennie, then to us and then to Independent Options.

Now that we had the person specification and the job description, we needed to advertise the post. The advert introduced Jennie, used information about what people appreciate about her from her person-centred plan, and information from the 'Matching Staff' tool. Jennie had her own car so a full clean driving licence was an 'essential' requirement. It was also important to me that women only supported Jennie as she has a lot of intimate personal care needs. We also wanted the advert to be clear that the Circle was commissioning Independent Options. See Figure 8.3 for what the advert looked like.

Individual Service

Person Specification for Jennie's support

Matching staff

Personality characteristics needed	Support needed	Skills needed for the post (essential requirements)	Shared interests (desirable requirements)
• Punctual • Adaptable • Calm • Patient • Good listener • Trustworthy • 'Firm but fair' approach • Confident • Good sense of humour • Positive attitude • Self-motivated • Confident • Leadership skills • Organisational skills **All assessed using the application form, activity interview and panel interview**	• To support Jennie in her weekly activity, going with her to all activities and supporting her in them • To communicate with Jennie using visual supports and her communication charts • To support Jennie in her friendships and relationships • To work with Jennie's family and Trust Circle to share and record information and learning • To support Jennie in her daily routines • To support Jennie with her person care needs • To help Jennie maintain a healthy lifestyle • To support Jennie in using the support plan and person-centred plan • To support Jennie by giving positive encouragement as well as setting firm boundaries when necessary • To support Jennie to manage her own home • To support Jennie be safe within the home and outside	• Good communication skills, using visual supports to do this where appropriate. • Good interpersonal skills and ability to relate well to others • Able to deliver flexible, sensitive support working to Jennie-centred plan, in a consistent way • Able to write accurate reports • Able to use a computer including Microsoft Office • Able to assist in the planning and budgeting of menus and meals • Able to work in a firm but fair approach • Personal commitment to valuing and respecting people's rights, choices and dignity • Able to carry out domestic tasks and managing finances • Able to satisfy an Enhanced CRB disclosure • Able to work as part of a team • Able to use own initiative • Personal flexibility and ability to work days, evenings, waking nights, sleep in duties, weekends and bank holidays on a rota system • Able to motivate self and others • Minimum of 2 years' experience working with people with learning disabilities and/or autism • Car driver with clean driving licence **Assessed using application form, group interview, activity interview and panel interview**	• Horse riding • Walking • Going to the gym • Cinema • Art activities • Bowling • Using a computer, for example using You Tube • Music (80s pop music) • Trampolining • Go to places of interest, for example Chester Zoo **Assessed using the application form and activity interview** Other desirable requirements • Previous experience of supporting people with autism • Knowledge of the Stockport area • NVQ level 3 in Health and Social Care • Experience of supervising staff • Experience of maintaining a staff rota • Ability to support individuals with their finances **Assessed using application form and panel interview**

Figure 8.1 Extracts from the job description for Jennie's Senior Support Worker

	Core responsibilities	Use judgement and creativity
Responsibilities to Jennie	1. To communicate well with Jennie. This means knowing how to communicate with Jennie and how Jennie communicates, and to use her communication system and visual cues daily (described in detail in her person-centred plan). 2. To support Jennie in her decision-making, so that Jennie increases the amount of choice and control that she has in her life. 3. To support Jennie in her relationships (for example, arranging for Jennie to meet up with her friends, supporting Jennie to send birthday cards) and enabling her to be part of her local community. 4. To support Jennie in all the activities on her weekly timetable and discuss any suggested changes with Suzie (Jennie's mum). 5. To work in a person-centred way with Jennie, going at her pace, supporting her to develop her interests. This may include practical assistance, support, teaching, advice, role modelling, encouragement and positive feedback. 6. To support Jennie to eat healthily and stay safe (there is detailed information about this in her person-centred plan). 7. To support Jennie in a respectful, dignified way. Her personal care routines are described in her person-centred plan. 8. To support Jennie in managing her own home, including domestic duties, paying bills, shopping, cooking and budgeting. 9. To have a positive, enabling and thoughtful agreed approach to enabling Jennie to take reasonable.	1. Helping Jennie to meet new people, establish new relationships, and be part of her local community. 2. Supporting Jennie to try new activities that she may enjoy (based on what we know is important to Jennie and how to support her).

Figure 8.2 Extracts from the job description for Jennie's Senior Support Worker

Figure 8.3 The advert for Jennie's staff

Sharing decision-making and the interviews

I think Independent Options was a bit surprised that we wanted to do everything ourselves and not use their standard job description or advert. We knew that the way we wanted to work was very new for any organisation, so decided to invite Jennie's Service Manager to a Circle meeting to look at how we could make decisions together about who to recruit. We worked with the Service Manager to put together a decision-making agreement specifically about recruitment, so that it was clear that Jennie and the Circle would make the final decision on who to appoint. This included deciding that I would shortlist with Joanne, and Jennie and Circle members would meet the shortlisted candidates (doing art together – an important part of Jennie's life) before the formal interviews (see Figure 8.4).

I shortlisted candidates with Joanna, the team manager, and we sent Jennie's one-page profile and 'perfect week' to the people we wanted to interview. The interview questions were based around this, and how people would deliver the support Jennie needed to achieve her 'perfect week' (see Figure 8.5). Like the job description, the interview questions were set out in order of responsibilities – to Jennie, to the Circle and then to the organisation.

Area of Jennie's life	How Jennie must be involved	Circle's role in decision-making	Independent Options' role in decision making	When and where the decision is made	How the final decision is made (consensus or who has the final decision-making responsibility)
Recruiting staff	Meeting people before the formal interview	To contribute to the job description, person specs and advert, ensuring that they reflect Jennie's person-centred plan To contribute to the interview questions, to include questions directly relating to Jennie's plan and scenarios from Jennie's life Circle members to be part of the panel and decision making	To finalise the job description, person specs and adverts to ensure they fit requirements of the organisation/law	Working on job descriptions etc. done through email according to recruitment timetable Decision on staff made as part of panel process after interview	Circle needs to sign off the final versions (Suzie and Helen) Circle members have the casting vote in interviews (Suzie)
Moving from waking nights to sleep ins		To review the learning logs from the waking night staff To review what is working and not working from Jennie's perspective, staff and the Circle's To suggest ideas for moving on, in ways that work for Jennie, and at her pace	To review the learning logs from the waking nights To contribute to what is working and not working from staff and managers' views	At a meeting between Suzie and Jo, or at a Circle meeting with Jo present At the 6-weekly and 3-monthly review with care manager	Consensus

Figure 8.4 Our decision-making agreement with Independent Options

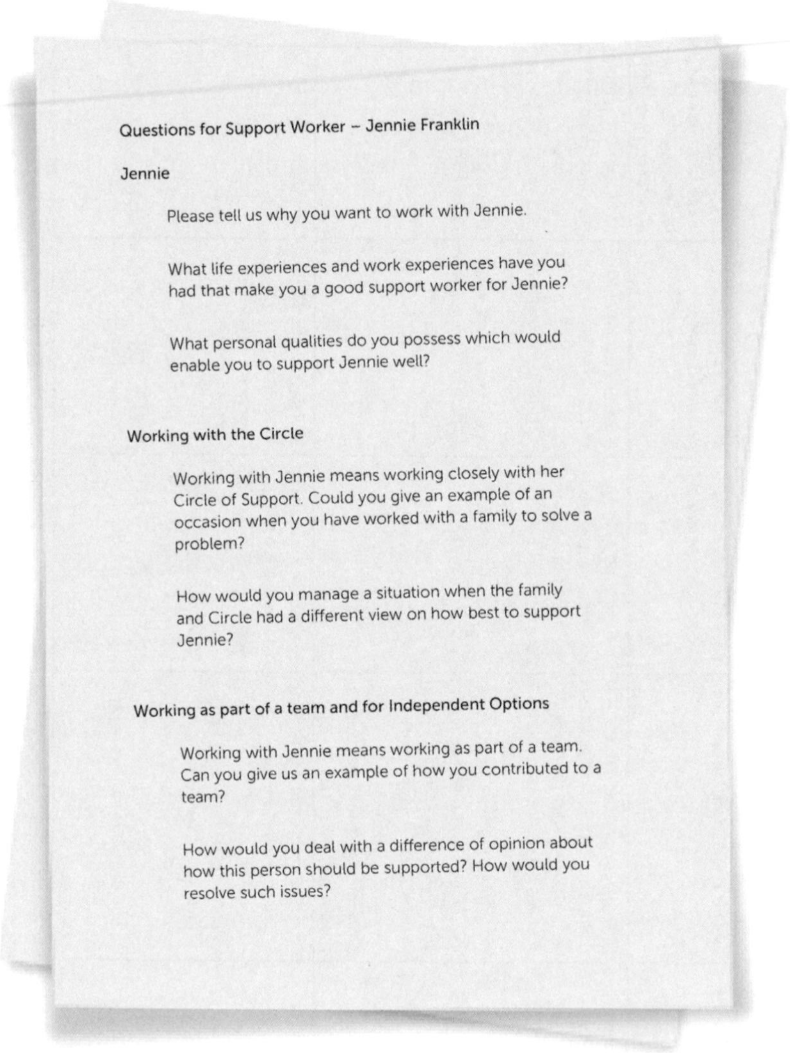

Questions for Support Worker – Jennie Franklin

Jennie

Please tell us why you want to work with Jennie.

What life experiences and work experiences have you had that make you a good support worker for Jennie?

What personal qualities do you possess which would enable you to support Jennie well?

Working with the Circle

Working with Jennie means working closely with her Circle of Support. Could you give an example of an occasion when you have worked with a family to solve a problem?

How would you manage a situation when the family and Circle had a different view on how best to support Jennie?

Working as part of a team and for Independent Options

Working with Jennie means working as part of a team. Can you give us an example of how you contributed to a team?

How would you deal with a difference of opinion about how this person should be supported? How would you resolve such issues?

Figure 8.5 Example interview questions

We conducted the interviews in three stages. First, candidates were invited to a group interview with the Circle and Independent Options. I introduced Jennie to the group by doing a presentation on how she would need supporting. Joanna did a presentation about Independent Options and then candidates were given tasks to do separately and in small groups. It was a good way of observing people's strengths and how they interacted. We then jointly agreed who to invite for a panel interview where we questioned candidates individually. From there we invited some of the candidates back again, by which time we felt we were getting the best of the best. This was for an informal interview involving Jennie as we wanted to see how they interacted with her and vice versa. It meant that if there was a close call between two candidates but Jennie made it clear that she liked one more than the other, or if someone demonstrated really good communication skills with Jennie and she responded happily, this could be the deciding factor. It was amazing to watch Jennie in these 'interviews' because she was interacting with people she had never met before. We had them all doing something that was important to Jennie – art.

The first recruitment phase was in November 2009 and we hoped to appoint the whole team (one senior, four support workers and two sessional workers to cover holiday, training and sickness, etc.) but we only found one support worker, which was really disappointing. Fortunately for us we recruited someone who was a real gem but we were all dissatisfied with the quantity and quality of some applications. It was really worrying because I knew that even though Jennie had this gorgeous flat, it wouldn't work without the right people around her. It was the beginning of a difficult time for me as I knew we had to recruit a great team fairly quickly because Jennie would have to move as soon as the flat was ready in order to claim housing benefit and the additional income support payment for her mortgage.

As a Circle we agreed to set up a transition team to support Jennie to move into her flat while we recruited the rest of the team; it wasn't ideal but we had to do something to ensure Jennie could move into the flat. Jennie's dad agreed to be part of this team with our one support worker but we still didn't have a senior support worker. I asked Jennie's Service Manager whether someone I'd met in another supported living service provided by Independent Options could be seconded to the team. Luckily for us all she agreed to move over to set the team up and support Jennie to settle in. It was stressful but ended up working really well. And after another round of recruitment we finally had Jennie's team in place.

At this stage we also finalised our contract with Independent Options for Jennie's service (see Figure 8.6). With a new team in place we could turn our thoughts to their training to become 'Jennie experts'.

For anyone else thinking about doing this I would say you know your child best so think about what is important to them. When you are choosing staff, match all those personality characteristics and interests together because then you are halfway there.

Individual Service Agreement

This agreement is the document that tells you about the service Independent Options will provide for you.

1. Parties to the Agreement

You:

Jennie Franklin

Your representative:

Jennie's Circle of Support -
Suzie Franklin, Dave Budsworth, Derek Franklin,
Matt Franklin, Helen Sanderson, Julie Bray and
Debbie Waters

Service Provider:

Independent Options (North West)

The Manager responsible for your service:

Joanna Babych

Figure 8.6 Extracts from our contract with Independent Options

9
Training and supporting staff to be 'Jennie experts'

Our newly recruited staff team quickly needed to become familiar with both Jennie and autism in a wider sense. We used the budget flexibly to provide training and support.

We agreed the induction programme with Independent Options to enable Jennie's new staff team to become 'Jennie experts'. Initially I was reluctant to lead the autism training because I wanted the support team to see me as Jennie's mum. However, I realised that it would be a wasted opportunity not to lead the training because it is what I do professionally and, as Jennie's mum, I am an expert in Jennie too.

We used Jennie's ELP as a starting point for Jennie-specific training and the team spent time with me and Jennie to understand why she did certain things and behaved in certain ways. They learned how to communicate with Jennie and how to support her to keep her anxiety levels down, because the better you can do this, the fewer difficulties there are to manage.

We also used some money from Jennie's personal budget in a creative way to pay for the team to have autism-specific training together and Jennie's dad and I stepped in to support Jennie to allow them all to attend as a team.

Visual timetables

Jennie has visual supports in her flat in the form of timetables and Social Stories™. There is a weekly timetable that uses photos to show Jennie all the activities she will be doing on each day, which members of staff will be with her, and when she will see me and her dad. The timetable reflects Jennie's 'perfect week' and is changed every Sunday so that Jennie can see the week ahead.

Visual prompts are used for chores such as making the bed and washing up, as well as for personal hygiene. For example, as well as a visual schedule to show Jennie how to clean her teeth, she has a two-minute digital timer so she knows she has to keep cleaning for that length of time. We have made little video clips of Jennie doing things 'properly' with me at home, including cleaning her teeth and washing, so that if she needs extra prompting the staff can show her the clip on her laptop.

Jennie can be obsessive about food and quickly put on weight as a teenager. She can become anxious about food and worries when she can eat next so everyone has to support Jennie to have a healthy diet and manage her portion sizes. The team uses a clear visual schedule for what she can eat and when: for example, she has a snack cupboard with healthy choices that she can choose from at snack times.

Jennie has a visual sleep schedule for a routine designed to calm her down before bedtime and help her sleep well. At bath time there are candles, colour-changing lights and classic FM playing on her iPad to relax her. Afterwards she is encouraged not to jump around and she goes to bed with a weighted blanket to meet some of her sensory needs.

Concerns

Jennie is a joy to be with most of the time but when she is very anxious her behaviour can deteriorate. This means that at times it is really exhausting to support her so I was concerned that the team might find working with Jennie harder than they expected. If this happened I was worried that there would be a high staff turnover, which would make life tough for Jennie as she would have to deal with more changes.

To combat this we had given the team a really good picture of Jennie, through the training, her ELP and her one-page profile, so they could understand her and really get to grips with her needs. We made it a very Jennie-specific process and by easing them in and having them shadow me and her dad it really seemed to help. I think the staff felt supported and valued, so my concerns, while rational and understandable, haven't come to fruition. In fact, it has been quite the opposite as they clearly love working with Jennie and have all overcome some difficult moments with professionalism and a clear desire to support her well.

Probation

We agreed with Independent Options at the beginning that the Circle would have the final say in recruiting someone and also their probationary period. At the end of the probationary period, the Circle talked about their experience of the staff and I fed this back to the manager, Joanna, for the end-of-probationary review. We adapted the job description by adding a column for our feedback on what was working and not working from our perspective, and what was working and not working from the staff member's perspective (see Figure 9.1).

Support worker

Core responsibilities	What is going well?	What needs to be improved?
To communicate well with Jennie. This means knowing how to communicate with Jennie and how Jennie communicates, and to use her communication system and visual cues daily (described in detail in her person-centred plan). To support Jennie in her decision-making, so that Jennie increases the amount of choice and control that she has in her life.		
Support Jennie in her relationships (for example, arranging for Jennie to meet up with her friends, like Rhian, supporting Jennie to send birthday cards) and enable her to be part of her local community.		
Support Jennie in all the activities on her weekly timetable and discuss any suggested changes with Suzie (Jennie's mum).		
Work in a person-centred way with Jennie, going at her pace, supporting her to develop her interests. This may include practical assistance, support, teaching, advice, role modelling, encouragement and positive feedback.		

Core responsibilities	What is going well?	What needs to be improved?
To support Jennie to eat healthily and stay safe (there is detailed information about this in her person-centred plan).		
Support Jennie in a respectful, dignified way. Her personal care routines are described in her person-centred plan.		
To support Jennie in managing her own home, including domestic duties, paying bills, shopping, cooking and budgeting.		
To have a positive, enabling and thoughtful agreed approach to enabling Jennie to take reasonable risk.		

Figure 9.1 Extract from the probationary review form

I gave Joanna my perspective on the relationship that different team members had with Jennie – the most important issue as far as the Circle was concerned. Joanna did the same, and in the review asked each individual what they thought was working and not working. Therefore, like a 360-degree appraisal, the review was based on information about each person's relationship with Jennie, and what was working and not working against the job description from my (and the Circle's) perspectives, the manager's perspective and the team member's.

This is the most important part of the whole process as far as I'm concerned. Getting the 'right' staff is absolutely crucial to any service working, from the person being supported to the team working well together. If you get this right the rest will fall into place.

> We were worried that staff would find Jennie exhausting at times. To combat this we gave the team a really good picture of Jennie through the training so they could really get to grips with her communication and understand her. We made it a very Jennie-specific process and by easing them in and having them shadow us, it really seemed to help.

10

Making it all happen – person-centred reviews and change

At last Jennie could move into her own home! It was an anxious time for the family as she made that transition but, after our careful preparation, it went remarkably well. We were prepared to meet challenges of course, but some were unexpected. We also had to learn how to support the staff in a person-centred way.

The respite service and direct payment continued until Jennie moved into her flat in April 2010. Unbelievably, all the transitions that I had been worrying about ended up going smoothly – school to college, college to flat, and children's services to personal budget. Even so, it was still very hard work making it happen while ensuring that the services stayed the same even though the funding systems differ between children's and adults' services. It was initially difficult to engage adult social care. We wanted them to be involved at reviews from when Jennie was about 16 so they could start planning their support and budgets well ahead of time. They did eventually start the transition process with us, albeit a little late, and have been great since.

The six months before Jennie moved in and the first six months in her new home were the most stressful for me. It was a whirl of regular meetings with various people and the Circle, sorting out Jennie's personal budget and the unexpected things we had to iron out, applying to the Court of Protection, securing Jennie's mortgage, liaising with solicitors and Johnnie Johnson Housing Trust, finding the right service provider, recruiting Jennie's team, furnishing the flat and moving her in. It took a huge amount of time and emotional energy to drive the process forward but with support from the Circle we made this work. After Jennie's move, life was very 'full on', and watching Jennie coming to terms with the changes was very emotional at times as she needed a lot of reassurance. For the first week I stayed with Jennie all the time, by the second week her staff were shadowing me and then in the third week they were doing more of the support and I was starting to go home at night.

This is when my anxiety levels rocketed because I was thinking 'What if something happens, will they know what to do?' but I quickly began to trust that they could manage situations. It took a while for me to feel relaxed as it was such a huge change for Jennie and all of us.

Life for Jennie now is fantastic – she is enjoying her independence and is incredibly happy most of the time, which is a delight and a relief for me to see. Jennie had a few difficult months settling in… and so did I letting go. It was a test for her and a test for her staff because they were all getting used to each other, but I couldn't have asked for it to have gone better. It is wonderful seeing her with her staff team; they all clearly love spending time with her and enjoy her 'perfect week' together. She has a really happy, active life and is supported by great people, some only a couple of years older than her, so it's as if she has best friends or big sisters. You can clearly see how the staff love her to bits.

If you had told me ten years ago this would have happened I would never have believed it. I was worried that she might be in an institutional setting or in supported living with people she didn't like or, worse still, didn't choose to live with.

> *Jennie had a few difficult months settling in…and so did I letting go. It was a test for her and a test for her staff because*

they were all getting used to each other, but I couldn't have asked for it to have gone better. It is wonderful seeing her with her staff team.

Person-centred reviews

Now we keep learning and adapting through the six-monthly person-centred reviews and regular Circle meetings. Julie, from the Circle, facilitates the person-centred reviews, using the same format as we did when Jennie was at school. We look at what is working and not working from everyone's perspective – Jennie's, the family's, the Circle's and the staff team's. The reviews are a great way to keep taking stock, updating Jennie's support plan and person-centred information, and working together to iron out problems and celebrate what is going well. We make sure we stay focused on outcomes and how we are using Jennie's budget to achieve these.

Challenges

Learning how to work with a provider, and the provider learning to work with us, has been quite a steep learning curve. We didn't always agree and had to keep developing our decision-making agreement and clarifying roles and responsibilities. One example was related to our Christmas meal and Independent Options' policy on staff boundaries. The Circle invited Jennie's staff team to join us for a meal at Christmas. Independent Options' professional boundaries policy states that staff who were not on duty were not allowed to have a drink with us. This did not make sense to us, as we felt we were inviting them to come and celebrate with us in their own time. This is an occasion where we had to agree to disagree with their policy.

Another issue was trying to understand their invoices. We are working with them to try to make these more family friendly, but there is still a little way to go.

Sometimes, we have to gently remind them that we are the commissioners of the service – their customers – and need to be seen and treated as such.

Overall, we have been very pleased with the way we can work together on issues. I think this will get better over time for families, as providers get used to seeing families and individuals as customers, purchasing their services with their budgets.

> *Learning how to work with a provider, and the provider learning to work with us, has been quite a steep learning curve. We didn't always agree and had to keep developing our decision-making agreement and clarifying roles and responsibilities.*

Developing as a person-centred team

We wanted to make sure that Jennie's service was the most person centred it could be. This meant making sure that the staff were supported in a person-centred way too. Around the same time, Helen's organisation, HSA, produced a self-assessment tool for managers, about person-centred support, called *Progress for Providers for managers*.[1] We agreed with Jennie's Service Manager that Julie would support the senior support worker to complete *Progress for Providers*, and we would then use that to support her to develop further. This gave us a 'baseline' starting point about how person centred Jennie's service was then, for us to build from. Julie then worked with the senior support worker to develop one-page profiles for each staff member, and looked at 'person-centred supervision'.

Making sure that staff are well supported, have regular team meetings and individual supervision about every six weeks is crucial to Jennie getting good person-centred support. We talked to Independent Options about making sure that the senior support worker had time on the rota to work alongside staff and coach

---

1   Helen Sanderson Associates (2011) *Progress for Providers – Checking Your Progress in Using Person Centred Approaches (Managers)*. Stockport: HSA Press. Available at: www.hsapress.co.uk/publications/books.aspx.

them. I recommend that you look carefully at the amount of time a manager spends with staff and the amount of time they spend in an office, away from the staff, and that the balance makes sense to you.

We were lucky that we had expertise in the Circle to use *Progress for Providers* to support and develop the staff team. However, any family could use *Progress for Providers* with the manager and staff they employ. It is easy to use and there are resources to help too.

Circle meetings

Now at the Circle meetings we invite the senior support worker to tell us how everything is going with the team in how they are supporting Jennie, in addition to the person-centred reviews. The first time Zoe did this, she presented it like a newspaper feature, sharing Jennie's support in a very positive way!

In the next chapter, we bring the story up to date.

11

Two years on – a new PATH

By summer 2012 the Circle and Jennie's team felt it would be a good time to complete another PATH with Jennie. Her life had changed so much since the original PATH that had led to her having her own home and team to support her. Doing a new PATH also confronted us with the long-term sustainability of Jennie's Circle.

We invited everyone in the Circle and Jennie's team to our house to work on the new PATH. Jennie was the star of the evening as usual and enjoyed being the centre of attention; she even drew and wrote on the pin boards for the first time, contributing circles in yellow to the PATH, making it hers.

One thing that came out of this discussion was to explore opportunities to support Jennie to contribute to the community she is living in. Reflecting on what is important to Jennie, we talked about the possibility of her doing some dog walking on a voluntary basis. She is now doing this with a dog called Charlie. We also wanted to explore setting up a social enterprise with other local young people where Jennie could make greetings cards and frame her art work to sell, as she is really creative and loves doing this. Last month I was a very proud mum when she exhibited her art-work in a local show.

We also talked about the long-term sustainability of the Circle and decided to work towards getting new and younger people involved to ensure it continues into the future and for the rest of

Jennie's life. This will involve changing some things around, sharing the responsibility of managing Jennie's money and accounts.

It was good to have some of Jennie's team at the PATH planning meeting as they were able to contribute ideas to reflect Jennie's new and independent life in her flat. They would like to be able to support Jennie to go on holidays abroad and we looked at how and when this may be possible. Jennie loves her holidays so this will definitely be something to work on with her team supporting her, rather than just her family.

We all agreed that Jennie's new PATH, which sets out what we want to have achieved by 2014, feels positive, inspiring and exciting (see Figure 11.1). Writing this book about our experiences was something that we also thought about on the new PATH. This book is a way to share what we have learned with Jennie.

What next?

For the future, I just want Jennie to remain happy and settled with great support from her team and Independent Options. With all the ideas the Path has come up with there's no doubt that Jennie will continue to have a fun-filled but purposeful life! I am a lot less worried about the future now. I feel I have done my best for Jennie; she has her independence and even when I am not here I know the Circle will carry on, ensuring that she lives a happy and fulfilled life.

Supporting Jennie to move in to her own home and setting up her team has not been easy. But if we can do it, I hope other families can be inspired by what we have achieved. We summarise what we learned as advice for families in the next chapter. I think there should be some responsibility on local authorities and service providers to make the process an easier one, and I hope they find it useful as well. We end the book with advice from us, and from other family leaders, for families, schools, providers and local authorities.

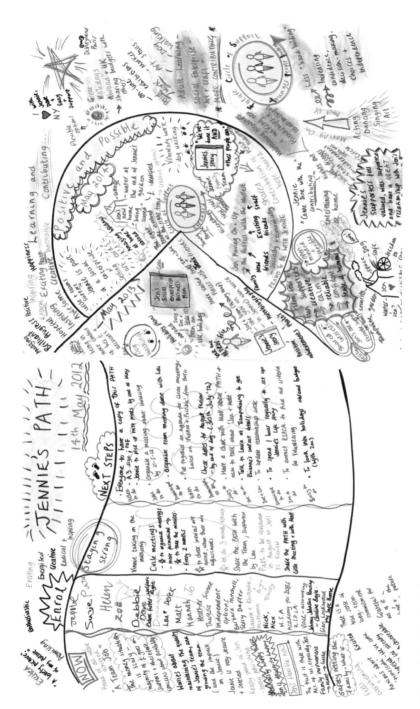

Figure 11.1 Jennie's Path

Finally, how Jennie's story helped to create change

Jennie does not know it but she became an inspiration to Dimensions, one of the country's largest service providers for people with learning disabilities and autism. Some years ago, Dimensions asked Helen Sanderson to support them through the seismic shift from traditional practice to more personalised support provision for families using personal budgets. Helen talked about her experience in the Circle and shared Jennie's story to illustrate how one family saw the possibilities and what they wanted to be in place to support their daughter.

Such was the impact of Jennie's story that, to help them change their services, the Dimensions managers asked of every process, policy and plan, 'Would that work *for Jennie?*' They wrote about that experience in their award-winning book *Making it Personal: A Provider's Journey from Tradition to Transformation* (listed under the resources on page 112). Using Jennie's story as a reality check worked for Dimensions. We hope Jennie can inspire other providers too.

Just as we were finishing the book we learned how Jennie is helping to make a difference where she lives as well. An action from her last person-centred review was to send a letter from Jennie to the other residents where she lives to explain a little bit about her and why they may hear her from time to time. We received a wonderful response from one of them and here is a little of what they said: 'I don't think you realise how important you are and I am being totally honest… We your neighbours should be lucky to have the pleasure to live in the same community as you…You should be the teacher and we are the ones who need to know how to live with you, not you how to live with us.'

> *Supporting Jennie to move in to her own home and setting up her team has not been easy. But if we can do it, I hope other families can be inspired by what we have achieved.*

12
Our advice for families, schools, providers and local authorities

I have shared some of my advice and suggestions throughout the book, and here we make some suggestions for families, schools, providers and local authorities. We developed these with other family leaders, and if all this could be in place, transition would be easy for everyone!

For families

- Think about what your dreams and fears and nightmares for the future are. Knowing what life you don't want for your child is a pretty good place to start and by writing these down it helps you move away from the nightmares and focus on the dreams.

- Don't panic – take small steps. The whole thing can be pretty overwhelming, so look at the things you need to know now and park the rest for later.

- Find out about person-centred planning – there are books, websites and courses that can help.

- Know your rights and their rights. Find out about the Mental Capacity Act and learn about what benefits your child may be entitled to in their own right. (Mencap has some useful factsheets to start with, www.mencap.org.uk/all-about-learning-disabilities/resources-centre.)

- Get people around you if you can – be prepared to ask for help, and consider circles of support.

- Connect with other families, for support, to problem solve together and to share ideas and learning.

- Think about how you can maximise the impact for your family (and others too). Is it by being a school governor? Or a carer forum rep? Perhaps you could work with the council representing carers/families? How can you get in there and make the changes at the level you want and need?

- Ask for and expect annual person-centred reviews for your child.

- Be prepared to 'drive' the process yourself if the school isn't. The process starts with schools and they sometimes only focus on education rather than the bigger picture. Always keep the bigger picture in mind – you're planning for the whole of your chils's life not just college. A person-centred review is a good place to start.

- Develop a one-page profile for your child and share it with the school or college, or do it with them if possible.

- Think about the support that you need to stay strong. You might want to consider a circle of support just for you. Have a look at *Five Ways to Well-being* as a place to start with building your own resilience (New Economics Foundation, www.neweconomics.org/publications/entry/five-ways-to-wellbeing).

- Know what 'good' looks like. For example, know what levels 4 and 5 are in the self-assessment tool *Progress for Providers* for managers, and *be prepared* to ask for that!

- Think about what a good future looks like and focus on life outcomes.

Useful resources

- www.personalisingeducation.org – provides examples of one-page profiles in schools.

- www.bit.ly/10ujVrU – this short film is useful for learning about person-centred reviews and what to expect (and what good looks like).

- www.bit.ly/11U4Vod – this animate on YouTube is a good one to start with to learn about one-page profiles.

- http://onepageprofiles.wordpress.com – provides examples of one-page profiles.

- www.thinkandplan.com – this is a resource on person-centred thinking tools.

- www.preparingforadulthood.org.uk – this is a great website for information about how to support young people to move into adulthood with choice and control and good life outcomes (employment, independent living, good health, friends, relationships and community inclusion). It describes national good practice.

- www.progressforproviders.org – this is where you can look at the different *Progress for Providers* self-assessments. You should look for providers that are using this and scoring 3 or more.

- http://onepageprofiles.wordpress.com – The one for families website was started by two parents of young children with learning disabilities to provide practical, positive information and tools which place families in control. Whilst aimed at families with children who have additional needs, much of the information and tools can be used by, and can benefit, all families.

- Gitsham, N. and Sanderson, H. (2011) *Getting a Job, Getting a Life and Getting it Right: Six Ways to Support Young Disabled People into Work*. Young disabled people can and do want to work. Having a job is a crucial part of leading a fulfilling life, yet very few adults with learning disabilities in the UK are in paid employment. So what does it take to help young disabled people get a job and get a life? Available from HSA Press: www.hsapress.co.uk/publications/books.aspx.

- http://aspirationsforlife.org – Aspirations for Life website has just been revamped and has some great tips and resources.

- www.community-circles.co.uk – this has information on circles of support.

- Early Support. *Family file* – a set of templates for families to fill in so that they don't have to tell their story repeatedly. Download free from www.ncb.org.uk/media/528046/family_file_-_main_document.pdf.

For schools

- Develop one-page profiles for each child so that everyone knows what is important and how to support them.

- Invest in annual person-centred reviews in all schools.

- Work in partnership with parents when additional support is needed for their child, such as jointly interviewing assistants or recruiting personal assistants who can work across home and school.

- Provide real work experience that is matched to the young person and their aspirations, and include Saturday jobs.

- Help raise the aspirations of what is possible among both young people and parents.

Resources

- personalisingeducation.org – provides examples of how schools are using person-centred practices and implementing one-page profiles, and blogs by teachers.

- http://aspirationsforlife.org – the aspirations for Life website has just been revamped and has some great tips and resources.

- www.preparingforadulthood.org.uk – this is a great website for information about how to support young people to move into adulthood with choice and control and good life outcomes (employment, independent living, good health, friends, relationships and community inclusion). It describes national good practice.

For providers

- Tell families what you can do, and give a menu of what you offer and what it costs. This could range from employing personal assistants on a family's behalf, to full Individual Service Funds, to providing management support to personal assistants that families employ.

- Invest in person-centred practices so that you can deliver the most person-centred services possible. Check your progress through using *Progress for Providers*.

- Think 'family-friendly' in everything you do – think about your 'customer journey' and what it would take to make this really work for families.

- Support families to do their one-page profile about what is important to and for them in terms of their relationship with you as a provider organisation.

- The easier and clearer things are, the better for everyone, for example contracts and invoices.

- Review everything regularly with families, for example, through person-centred reviews.

- Have a single point of contact for families.

- Remember that families are the new commissioners!

Resources

- www.bit.ly/11U4Vod – to learn about one-page profiles start with this animate about them on YouTube.

- http://onepageprofiles.wordpress.com – this provides examples of one-page profiles.

- www.thinkandplan.com – this is a resource on person-centred thinking tools.

- www.helensandersonassociates.co.uk – this is useful for learning about person-centred reviews.

- http://progessforproviders.org – this gives the full range of free self-assessments.

- Scown, S. and Sanderson, H. (2010) *Making It Personal: A Provider's Journey from Tradition to Transformation*. Stockport: Dimensions and HSA Press. Jennie features in this book that describes how a national provider, Dimensions, is starting to offer support to families and individuals who have personal budgets.

- Steve, S. and Sanderson H. (2011) *Making it Personal for Everyone: From Block Contracts towards Individual Service Funds.* Stockport: Dimensions and HSA Press. This book describes how a national provider, Dimensions, started to introduce Individual Service Funds.

- Bennett, S., Stockton, S., Sanderson, H. and Lewis, J. (2012) *Choice and Control for All: The Role of Individual Service Funds in Delivering Fully Personalised Care and Support.* London: Groundswell. This report summarises the learning to date about Individual Service Funds. Jennie's Circle is described as an example of good practice. www.groundswellpartnership. co.uk/choice-and-control-for-all.

- www.preparingforadulthood.org.uk – this is a great website for information about how to support young people to move into adulthood with choice and control and good life outcomes (employment, independent living, good health, friends, relationships and community inclusion). It describes national good practice.

For local authorities

Here are some of the important elements of this that we would encourage local authorities to consider, to make preparing for adulthood work for everyone.

- Help families tell their stories once only – through having a single assessment process, or supporting families to record their own person-centred information to share with professionals.

- Have one person to support families such as a key worker system, or a process such as Local Area Coordination.

- Take a whole-family approach and consider family budgets.

- Have one education, health and care plan, based on person-centred practices that includes a one-page profile for the young person and a one-page profile for the family.

- Provide families with information about what is possible, not just what is available.

- Invest in family leadership training and support, including training and support in person-centred practices.

- Make sure that families and young people can buy what they need with their personal budget, and can get support in getting a job, a home of their own and good support from providers or personal assistants. Develop a market of offerings to families and young people that they can buy from.

- Make sure that families can get a circle of support facilitator if they want one.

- Make support planning and signing off support plans as simple, easy and quick as possible.

- Co-produce strategic development in partnership with families, through processes like 'Working Together for Change', an eight-stage process that takes information from person-centred review to inform strategic change (Bennett, S., Sanderson, H. and Stockton, S. (2012) *Working Together for Change: Citizen-led Change in Public Services.* London: Groundswell. www.groundswellpartnership.co.uk/Working TogetherforChangecitizen-ledchangeinpublicservices).

Resources

- www.ncb.org.uk/early-support/resources/mapit-tool – the Early Support *Multi Agency Planning and Improvement Tool* can be downloaded here for free. It supports authorities to work effectively with other agencies.

- 'Working Together for Change', an eight-stage process that takes information from person-centred review to inform strategic change (Bennett, S., Sanderson, H. and Stockton, S. (2012) *Working Together for Change: Citizen-led Change in Public Services*. London: Groundswell. www.groundswell partnership.co.uk/WorkingTogetherforChangecitizen-led changeinpublicservices).

- Government guidance on how person-centred practices are important in delivering personalisation (Department of Health (2010) *Personalisation through Person-Centred Planning*. London: Department of Health. http://webarchive. nationalarchives.gov.uk/20130107105354/http://www. dh.gov.uk/prod_consum_dh/groups/dh_digitalassets/@ dh/@en/@ps/documents/digitalasset/dh_115249.pdf).

- www.preparingforadulthood.org.uk – this is a great website for information about how to support young people to move into adulthood with choice and control and good life outcomes (employment, independent living, good health, friends relationships and community inclusion). It describes national good practice, policy and stories.

- http://aspirationsforlife.org – the Aspirations for Life website has just been revamped and has some great tips and resources.

AFTERWORD

This is a powerful story, and Suzie's success in enabling her daughter Jennie to live a full life is due to a number of factors. Her story speaks of the importance of good person-centred information; having choice and control though personal budgets; having people around to support you; having high aspirations of what is possible;, and of providers being prepared to change and see the family as the commissioner. This echoes the aspirations of many families in Stockport, who have worked with a wide range of partners to describe the experiences that they want to see in place to support their children in their journey from birth to adulthood. We have looked at what is working and not working for children, families, staff and schools around transition. From this analysis, we asked families to tell us how they wanted their future to look.

We know that families want to tell their stories once, and for this to be recorded in a person-centred way, as it was in Jennie's had with her person-centred plan. This shared vision includes one-page profiles, that grow and change with the child, and are used throughout school. Jennie was the first young person to have a person-centred review in Stockport, and we want this this extended to everyone. Circles also feature in our vision for the future, as one way to offer long-term support to families. We want everyone to have high aspirations for young people, to live, work and thrive in their communities, with many options for paid work that include microenterprises, and internships, good housing solutions, and providers offering truly person-centred support.

At the time of writing there is a Children and Families Bill working its way through Parliament. It includes a requirement that we will replace some of our cumbersome and bureaucratic processes with a single, holistic and comprehensive plan for our children with the most complex needs. This signals the start of a serious change in culture in which the journey of a child from birth to adulthood is underpinned by a continuous offer of support, rather than a series of sometimes disconnected assessments as a child develops. The real challenge to us is to achieve a response which is "'doubly holistic'" – that is, it provides continuity for the child over time, but at any point, achieves an integrated approach by all services to the child and family.

We are already working towards this culture change in Stockport, in partnership with families. We are co-producing these developments, and have made some significant steps forward. We are the first local authority to expect all young people to have a one-page profile, in primary, secondary and special schools. At the time of writing we are actively supporting a quarter of the schools in Stockport to achieve this, and will be extending this next year. As part of theis programme, we hope that all children with special educational needs will have support built around annual, person-centred reviews.

We are introducing a truly person-centred approach to the 0—25 plan, and one-page profiles and person-centred reviews are central to both creating and implementing these plans. Personal budgets for children and families are being introduced, and we are supporting a new third- sector initiative called Community Circles, whicho are is exploring ways to make cCircles, like Suzie and Jennie's, available to many more families. There is a lot to do, but we think we are making some good progress.

We need all families like Suzie and Jennie to have a positive experience of the transition to from school to adult life. We are working with families to try and to make that happen.

As President of the Association of Directors of Children's Services (ADCS) for the year 2013–20/14 I have been privileged to work closely with a number of key people in central government departments, with colleagues across the voluntary and independent sectors and with other local authorities. There is enormous commitment across the country, at all levels, to bring about a culture change in the way we identify strengths and needs, and provide support to children with additional needs and their families. Suzie's story reinforces my view that significant change should and can happen, and we must make it happen.

Andrew Webb

President of the Association of Directors of Children's Servces Ltd (ADCS) and Coporate Director, Services for People, Stockport Council.

APPENDIX

	What it does	How this tool helps	A quick glimpse
Sorting important to/for	Sorts what's important TO (what makes us happy, content, fulfilled) from what's important FOR (health and safety, being valued) while working towards a good balance.	As a way to think through a situation before deciding what should happen next. As an everyday tool. As part of reviews. As the beginning of an individual, family or team plan.	important TO / important FOR / need to learn/know
The doughnut sort	Identifies specific responsibilities - core responsibilities using judgement and creativity not a paid responsibility.	Helps you know where you can be creative without fear. It clarifies the roles of the different professionals and agencies supporting people and families. It can inform a family support plan. It clarifies roles and expectations in a team plan.	core responsibility; use judgement/creativity; Not our paid responsibility

Matching staff	A structure to look at both what skills/supports and what people characteristics make for good matches.	Helps people think about what kind of paid support they want and need. In recruiting team members. Gives the information for the characteristics section of a plan.
Relationship circle	Identify who is important to a person or family.	Learn who is important to people. See if there are any important issues around relationships. Helps identify who to talk to when developing a plan. Identify relationships that can be strengthened or supported.
Communi-cation charts	Helps us focus on people's communication whether they use words to speak or not.	A quick snapshot of how someone communicates. A way of recording a richness of information for people who use words to speak and particularly for people who don't.

Learning log	Directs people to look for ongoing learning. A structure that captures details of learning within specific activities and experiences. Provides a way of recording information which focuses on what needs to stay the same and what needs to be different around how we support people.	Provides a way for people to record ongoing learning (focused on what worked well, what didn't work well) for any event or activity. Tells us what is important to and for individuals, families and team plans. Can replace traditional notes or records to help us focus more clearly on critical information about the person. Can be used to focus on someone's whole life or specific areas of their life, e.g. someone's health, how people like to spend their time.	
Sorting what's working/not working	Clarifies what to build on (maintain or enhance) and what to change. Helps in looking at how: any part of a person's life is working, medications are working, people providing paid support are doing in their work, any effort, activity or project is working. Helps with mediation where there are disagreements.	Analyses an issue/situation across different perspectives. Provides a picture of how things are right now.	

INDEX